DESIGNING THE DESIGN FIRM

THE QUEST FOR HIGH-PERFORMANCE DESIGN

JAMES O. JONASSEN

DESIGNING THE DESIGN FIRM

THE QUEST FOR HIGH-PERFORMANCE DESIGN

JAMES O. JONASSEN

Library of Design Management

Greenway Communications

ISBN: 978-0-9846136-4-9

Östberg Library of Design Management
Greenway Communications, LLC
a division of the Greenway Group

25 Technology Parkway South, Suite 101
Atlanta, GA 30092

(800) 726-8603

www.greenway.us
www.di.net

For Marilyn

CONTENTS

PREFACE

The incentive for writing this book is a concern about the design profession that I have witnessed in more than 40 years of practice as an architect. If we do not improve our design performance, we will lose relevance and the ability to shape our environment positively. This is a concern for the professions of design but also for the choices that society will make without the help of strong design process.

What is the role of design in society to be?

This is one of the big challenges of the profession. Others have redefined themselves over time as society's needs have changed and broadened their role in the process. Most of the redefinition by architects has been to diminish the role, narrow the definition, and eschew risk and societal involvement — almost to the point of irrelevance.

The buildings we design house and therefore influence nearly all of the activities that produce gross national product for every country, and they impact the lives of those who use them and are around them. Buildings are responsible for about half of all energy consumption as well as consumption of a huge portion of renewable and nonrenewable resources. If we as designers are not consistently pursuing maximum return on that commitment of resource and impact on society, then we are behaving irresponsibly.

As designers, we have the ability to shape the environment in ways that benefit life on this planet at many levels beyond survival — in performance, healing, learning, creativity, and feeling, to name a few. Yet it is hard to find buildings that push the broad performance-improvement aspect of design, and it is rarely recognized in design award programs or publications. Maybe, and I hope this is true, there are more buildings that do this than is readily apparent simply because it is not a part of our design consciousness. But it should be.

Except for the issue of value consciousness, designers and particularly architects have enjoyed a relatively high level of trust from the public, while the images of other professionals have not been as accepted. Attorneys are not generally held in high esteem because of perceived self-interest above client well being, as is apparent in many class action lawsuits; physicians have an uneven image; trust in business leaders has diminished due to major events like the collapse of General Motors and the BP fiasco in the Gulf of Mexico; and certainly the recent economic collapse has all but dissolved any trust in bankers and brokers. But if designers do not address real value in the face of a growing awareness of the limits on resources, that trust will evaporate and, more important, those resources will continue to be squandered.

One of the bits of wisdom I picked up some years back (from Nancy Pearl, former Seattle head librarian, via my wife Marilyn) was a preservation-of-time rule to the effect that "You should not read more than your age in pages of a book that hasn't captured your interest." For the demographic that might open this book I think that would mean about 30 to 60 pages.

Let me help you shorten that decision time frame by telling you what to expect and what this book is not. This is a discussion of design practice focused on architecture and relating to practices addressing issues with multiple stakeholders. It poses a purpose for design that is a very high performance benchmark. It describes the need to design practices to pursue that purpose and means to shape a practice for that pursuit. It is a personal recollection of a 40-year (and ongoing) quest of my own firm and how we addressed designing our practice with ideas that worked and many that didn't, and also a look at other firms that are highly regarded, including specifically a handful of the best firms in Denmark.[1]

While this book reviews ideas that have been tried and gives my personal view on a lot of issues, none of these are answers for others who are designing their practices even though they may sound like it in many cases. (When they do,

---

[1] Why Denmark? In the Arcspace Web site list of well recognized architectural design firms, the Danes seem disproportionately represented: about 24 are from the United States, and 11 are Danish, yet Denmark's population (5.5 million) is less than my home state of Washington. Even allowing for a slight bias from the site's Danish-born editor-in-chief, this is disproportionate. Denmark seems to have a national ethos that is particularly advantageous to high-performance design:

- It is one of two countries in the world with a national policy on design (the Netherlands being the other)
- The fact that it has such a policy is a result of a tradition of appreciating and valuing design at the highest levels for a long time.
- The country has two very good and highly influential architectural design schools.
- It is an egalitarian, consensus based society, valuing curiosity and objectivity, to some extent the result of an 18th-century teacher/preacher named Grundtvig and the early 20th-century Prime Minister Stauning.
- It is a multi lingual country and a magnet for young designers from many parts of the world, thus infusing those firms open to it with a broad exposure to other cultures.

Profiles of these firms are included in the notes in the back of this book.

please be especially skeptical.) These are, however, many, if not most of the questions that need to be addressed and a body of experiences in the quest for creating a design firm consistently capable of high-performance design.

The major premises herein are these:

- Design, especially architecture, is for a positive purpose (including, but much more than, inspiring form).
- To achieve this effectively and efficiently, a design practice itself must be designed in a way that creates a habitat for high design performance, a characteristic I call high pH because it's all about people and habitat.
- The design and implementation of a high pH practice is a conscious, arduous, and never-ending quest.
- There are quite a number of interrelated sine qua non issues that must be successfully addressed in that design process, but here you will have to go to the text.

The format of the book is that the first chapters deal with making the case for the mandate; the chapters following deal with how to pursue the quest. Each of the "how" chapters leads with a description of the issues and relevant responses, then goes to a narrative of my personal experiences at NBBJ, and finally the chapter is capped with descriptions of six Danish design firms' responses to these issues.

INTRODUCTION: A PERSONAL PERSPECTIVE

Where it began

My father's Danish ancestors were mostly horticulturists, gardeners, and florists, and my father's first career was as a flower shop proprietor. But as a result of World War II, when sources of flowers dried up and military construction demand was high, he became a builder, as did his brother. All of my mother's family — my two uncles my grandfather, and several older cousins — were also builders. I had a hand in building from a very young age as I helped my father remodel from the ground up (rebuild, really) the house we lived in. Later, as a teenager, I worked at his construction company. My father was also an artist at heart and instilled in me, my elder sister, and younger brother an early appreciation of art and music.

With that background, it was not surprising that I knew I wanted to be an architect early on. I was awed by the works of Frank Lloyd Wright published in a couple of 1950s and '60s issues of *House Beautiful* magazine, and not a little swayed by my dad's perception that architects made a lot of money (and my perception that they drove cool cars).

While I was engaged in architecture school, I had a memorable argument with a slightly older cousin that caused me to think more critically about what architectural design was for. My cousin said that architects were dilettantes whose sole purpose was to make buildings look different … and difficult to build. I of course mounted the arguments from the architectural canon that I was learning at the time that architects exist to make buildings handsome and inspiring through appropriate and "honest" use of materials and structure as well as consideration of context. Even at the time I was not very satisfied with that argument and was disturbed that I didn't have a more meaningful definition of purpose for what I intuitively knew was important and to which I was emotionally committed.

That early challenge from someone important to me is where I believe my personal quest for significant purpose in architectural design began.

My college years at the University of Washington were heavily influenced by modernist as well as regionalist ideas from very good teachers and architects, including Fred Bassetti, Wendell Lovett, Keith Kolb, Ibsen Nelson, Rich Haag, and Victor Stienbrueck, to name a few. While that was inspiring regarding the search for handsome and contextually appropriate form, I was in search of purpose which went beyond that.

In graduate school at Columbia, I was attracted to the philosophy of Victor Christ-Janer, an architect who espoused a Jungian notion that there is universal (archetypal) meaning in architectural form that could be drawn on to design spaces that would shape or at least heavily influence human response and behavior. I did a year's research thesis on that topic with a very skeptical advisor. In the end I too was disappointingly skeptical. Even if I could find symbolic meaning, it was not where I was going to find meaningful purpose. But I did get a feel for purpose out of my design thesis, which was a mixed-use community center for central Harlem.

Once in practice at NBBJ, my outlook was molded by the experiences of real-world design practice. At first I had a singular focus on designing projects to fulfill the program needs expressed by clients with formal expression drawn from both modernist and regionalist influence. Then sequentially I began addressing what I encountered and perceived as external obstacles to uncompromised implementation of design — economic and operational consequences, cost, politics, and communication with clients. Dealing with those issues opened me to a broader definition of purpose.

Later, after I became a partner in the practice, I realized that issues of firm culture have a profound influence on design outcome, and if those are not optimized, the potential to get the best possible out of design is crippled. Within a couple of years of becoming a partner, I and several of my partners began the quest to achieve high-performance design consistently, even though we didn't call it that at the time.

The Quest

I am later going to say more about how architects' perspective on what is important in design is hugely shaped by the nature of their practice experience. Many feel that practice building may be necessary but is largely a waste of time for "real" architects and is better left primarily to business-oriented architects whose focus is not on the quality of architecture. The idea of designing a practice is not on the radar screen at all.

I argue, however, that if your experience goes beyond the intimacy of single individual clients into the realm of multi-stakeholder or program-driven projects, you quickly realize the importance of a designed approach, or the realization sneaks up on you as you witness disappointments in the final outcome of this kind of work. For me and my partners, this was the kind of work we were engaged in from the start even though each of us had had at least a taste of single-family or other small-project work while in school or with prior firms.

At the time I joined the firm in 1965, a transformation was underway, led by the only second-generation partner the firm has ever had, Bill Bain. He had come with a mission to achieve a more rigorous design agenda in a 20-year-old firm that had done reasonably well in design recognition but was more noted for its ability to deliver solid projects reliably. He strove to get younger designers, several recently out of Ivy League schools, in the design leadership of projects. This had the immediate impact of increasing excitement in the firm as well as the ratio of design awards and publication of work. At the same time, because of the divide it created between youthful design exuberance and seasoned (sometimes cynical) implementation experience, the realized projects were not all that they might have been. This was a big lesson in the importance of design team integration.

The first generation of partners somehow decided to pass on the legacy of their firm to future generations of architects. Their approach to this was never explained to me, but it appeared that they decided to make partners of all of the leading contributors to the firm at the time and allow them to sort out how to make it work. Within three or four years, the firm went from five partners to nearly 20. At age 29, I became one of this group of new partners.

This was a large increase in anointed leaders in a short period of time. These leaders were diverse in background, in age (20-somethings to 60-somethings) and, as it turned out, in values. Most felt individually entitled to determine direction for the firm. Though there was a clear legacy of ethical values, there was no clear agreement on purpose among this newer group of partners. Partner meetings seemed to be for the purpose of having them! It was not a productive time.

It was then that a few of us, whose main credentials were that we were among the young design leaders and were also bringing in a majority of the firm's work at the time, decided that we needed to design the practice to accomplish a coherent purpose. This began the quest that evolved to design a high-performance firm that could produce the best outcomes relevant to society's needs and requirements of the global ecosystem.

That quest has been going on ever since: a quest reviewed and renewed almost every year. We have looked for successful models to learn from and emulate in some cases, sought ideas about creativity from many sources, and designed and tried alternative structure, process, organization, ownership, reward systems, and decision making and direction setting approaches.

In the meantime, as I experienced extreme social inequities through working in places like the Philippines and have seen incredible resources gobbled up by heroic projects that do not accomplish concomitant good, my values have been shaped to include a strong aversion to both social inequity and excess in anything. This awareness helped evolve my views of purpose in design. My view was also shaped by working with incredible clients who demanded design for the soul and were concerned about impact on performance but who also had a deep concern about appropriate means.

What design — and particularly architectural design — should accomplish to justify the commitment of resources that it entails is a maximized positive effect using an economy of means. The positive effect must include moving human experience, which is currently recognized in the highest design recognition and honors programs, but it must also include performance improvement and, better yet, transformation for the enterprise involved. And it must achieve this with the least reasonable consumption of resources, renewable and non-renewable, including money and time. To differentiate this from what is most often recognized as great design, I call this high-performance design. And that is what we have been chasing at NBBJ.

Out of over 40 years' experience in this quest, I believe that design of a firm capable of consistently doing high-performance design can be achieved by doing a couple of obvious things:

- Bond the right people.
- Create a high-performance habitat.

Done well and together, these will produce what I call a high pH firm. Stretching both chemical and semantic analogies, a high pH firm is one that reacts powerfully to challenge, shares its charge readily, and is an incredible starting point for any undertaking.

Of course, attaining the right people is a challenge but one that can be met and is made easier by a high-performance habitat.

And, certainly, a high-performance habitat is nothing that will fall in your lap, but if you have the passion for it, it can be created. And, oh yes, the right people help create the habitat.

That people are key in design is no revelation, I am sure, but how they relate to one another and how their values and passions relate to the firm's *raison d'être* are critical to high design performance. And the people who matter are everyone — from owner/leader to receptionist/model maker.

In my mind, habitat includes culture, approach, and structure. An enterprise's culture includes its values, purpose, participation, and communication. Its approach is the attitude and methodology it brings to its projects and its practice. Structure includes team, context, support, leadership and ownership, and place.

1

THE MANDATE FOR HIGH-PERFORMANCE DESIGN

Designers have a responsibility to design for a positive purpose.

If you accept that, then consider that designers must also have the responsibility to achieve high-performance design, design that makes the most benefits from the resources it commits.

If you buy those ideas, then consider that designers must design their design firm, or enterprise, to be the most effective they can be at achieving high-performance design.

The reality seems to be, however, that very few design firms ever get around to designing their own practices for high performance.

That leads to the purpose of this book, which is an exploration of designing a firm or enterprise for high design performance, a characteristic I call high pH (encompassing people and habitat, defined in the Introduction and below).

By "firm" I mean the people and total habitat of structure, approach, and culture that undertake to design and realize physical intervention in our environment.

Whether or not you accept the first two considerations, you may feel that the third, design of the firm, is unnecessary, redundant, incomprehensible, or an obvious but trivial truth to be accomplished by managers and accountants. A lot of designers feel that way.

Whatever your opinions about design of the design firm for high design performance, you may find the discussion of the quest to achieve that interesting. Here are my definitions of these two terms:

High-performance design is design that:

- Awakens and inspires the human spirit
- Transforms the user enterprise to a higher level of performance
- Makes the place (or object) better than what went before it, including the context in which it resides
- Is accomplished with the minimum, essential, and sustainable resources
- Is affordable to the user enterprise and to society (in all resources, including time and money)

Is this real? It asks for a lot. It is hard to do and hard to find. In reviewing the projects on the Pritzker Prize Web site, I could not find any that clearly achieved a majority of these criteria, though part of the reason, I believe, is that much of this set of high-performance design criteria is simply not considered and therefore not documented. I trust that some of these projects, in fact, do meet my criteria. There is more documentation of this sort in the BusinessWeek/Architectural Record Awards program. I visited and reviewed two projects that won awards in that program that meet most of my criteria:

- The Saint-Hyacinthe School of Trades and Technologies in Quebec by ABCD Architecture-Urbanism, which transformed education in the trades to a new level of respect and recognition, created a great sense of community and aesthetic inspiration, made the building itself part of the learning experience, exceeded all performance goals (attracting enrollment, retaining faculty, etc.), and did it all with very modest means.
- The Valeo Technical Center (for design, testing, and production of original and aftermarket automotive parts) in Auburn Hills, Mich., by Davis Brody Bond, which helped the company integrate two previously independent entities (engine cooling and climate control), promoting cross-functional thinking and improved quality and efficiency. The owner's assessment of results showed improved communication, supplier and customer relationships resulting in across-the-board schedule, delivery and quality improvement, as well as increased success in recruiting and retaining top talent. This was done in a simple, elegant, transparent environment, visually uniting functions with wildly different environmental needs.

NBBJ has designed and implemented a number of projects that meet most of these criteria. Three of them are described in project plates beginning on page 122, and a couple of others include:

- The Boeing Company's Move to the Lake project in Renton, Wash., which helped create engineering and fabrication integration and a renewed sense of purpose and resulted in a reduction of production time for the 737 series aircraft from 22 days to 11. And this was done with a very modest set of interventions in the existing plant.

- The Joint Campus of the University of Washington and Cascade Community College in Bothell, Wash., which brought together two originally resistant faculties and administrations into a mutually beneficial environment, integrated the campus into a broader community, and restored a neglected wetland to a model habitat, teaching, and research environment while saving the state millions of dollars compared to a more conventional approach to campus making.

So my answer is: Yes, it is real.

In defining high-performance design, I do not want to give the impression that I think that the beauty, the soul, the awareness, and the sensory awakening aspects of design are secondary to any of the more pragmatic or economic aspects. Design must address form, tectonics, craft, color, light, texture, sound, reflection, and shadow. It must achieve a provocative relationship between simplicity and complexity. And it must access the unconscious. Or as Kenya Hara says: Design is information architecture, and "although the materials of that architecture's construction are indeed the information brought from the outside by the sensory organs, at the same time some very important building blocks are also the recollected experiences, the memories, awakened by these external stimuli".[2]

High-performance design must enrich the human experience beyond its pragmatic purpose or it will have fallen short and be a tragic waste. It cannot be an either/or approach, it must be both/and. A colleague has said (in a very American male way): "This is an unattainable goal ... the straight-A valedictorian ... captain of the football team ... student body president ... dating the head cheerleader." While I agree that this is a very demanding goal, I am also convinced that it is achievable, but only if it is taken seriously as a goal.

Now to define what the design firm needs to accomplish to pursue this.

---

[2] Hara, Kenya, *Designing Design*, Baden, Switzerland, Lars Muller Publishers, 2007.

High design performance (high pH):

- Consistently produces high-performance design
- Is inspiring for participants in the process
- Is both effective and efficient
- Is affordable to the user and society (in time and money)
- Is profitable to the design enterprise and financially equitable to the enterprise staff.

To design an enterprise for high design performance, the right people must be united and a habitat for creativity must be created. The result is what I call a high pH entity.

In the following pages I will make the case for design for positive purpose based on society's license of trust, service contract commitments, and man's mutual reliance on the environment; the case for high-performance design based on finite resources, renewable imperatives, and competitive survival; and the case for design of the design firm based on ideas about creativity and effectiveness.

2

THE CASE FOR POSITIVE PURPOSE

Many people think of design as primarily an issue of aesthetics and form (beautiful or handsome or interesting or inspiring), much as they think of art. Design by most definitions, however, has a purpose. I like "exquisite" as a characteristic of design because, unlike "beauty," which is defined as "exciting aesthetic pleasure," "exquisite" is defined as having "beauty, fitness, and perfection," thus incorporating aesthetics as well as purpose and high performance.

Michigan architect Alden B. Dow said it well more than 50 years ago in his essay in *Creativity and Its Cultivation*: "... if we are going to be creative, all we need is to develop a deep sense of care. First, however, we must have a purpose or a way of life that is commensurate with human needs." [3]

Architecture has the obvious purpose of shelter, intervening between buildings' inhabitants and nature, just as any product has its obvious purpose as an eating utensil, hammer, or whatever. The question of purpose is really one of establishing what else is important in designing such a thing and what the designer wants to achieve as a broader purpose. Yes, even a fork can have a broader purpose, such as accommodating impaired or small hands; imparting a sense of reverence, gravitas, or joy to the act of eating; using materials that are particularly sustainable or appropriate to the region of origin or use; or method of fabrication.

Vitruvius's oft-quoted (and inscribed on the Pritzker Medal) "Commodity, Firmness, and Delight" captures the purpose in commodity. A building is to accommodate some purpose.

There are, of course, some additional commitments to purpose that come with the architectural designer's role.

---

[3] Anderson, Harold H. editor, *Creativity and Its Cultivation*, New York, Harper & Row, 1959.

Social Contract

In many societies, architectural designers enjoy a privileged position of trust, giving them a monopoly, or at least hegemony,on the act of designing buildings that are likely to be used by the public. Most often the legislative reason for granting that monopoly is an exchange for accepting responsibility to protect the public safety and welfare. Safety is often well defined and for the most part prescriptively so. Welfare is usually more vaguely defined but is generally taken to include preservation of health through, clean air and water and a safe environment in terms of sound and light.

Service Contract

Contractual agreements between project sponsors (clients) and architects usually specify the architect's responsibility to the client, the point of which is to create a building suitable for the purpose intended. The specificity of that agreement is generally negotiated over time by associations of the interested parties and focuses primarily on establishing rules for dispute resolution.

For architects who begin their practices through design of single-family residences, which is true for many American architects, these two sets of demands on them as professionals likely seem to be a reasonable expression of total purpose:

Satisfy the client's expressed needs and desires functionally and aesthetically. Make the result safe.

These are the basic issues of purpose that are the sine qua non of professional practice of architecture (and essentially the same for industrial design, product design, interior design, etc.).

However, by virtue of their training in and their passion for design, designers are also deeply motivated to deliver something that is inspiring, original, and bearing their own sense of authorship.

And there are other expectations: those of clients about relevant and effective design and those of peers about upholding the reputation of the profession.

Client Expectations

Clients bring expectations to the design process shaped by their own experiences, enterprise goals and culture, and personal motivations. Not all clients are seeking high-performance design. Those who are most likely to seek it are those who want to use a building project (or a product) to transform their enterprise to a higher level of performance or their customers to a higher level of experience. Clients who are satisfied in a belief that they have already optimized their performance model in whatever their enterprise often are not interested in design that reaches for improvement.

Peer Expectations

Most designers have respect for their peers and care about their opinions. Respect and recognition are largely based on the work of the designer and the ethics demonstrated by the practice and in rarer cases by an admiration for the culture of the practice (often made apparent by the quality of people both leaving and returning to a firm).

Experience and Purpose Perspective

An architect's individual perspective on the purpose of design is shaped by the pedagogy encountered in school, and after that by the nature of practice experience. Examples of what I mean by practice experience include:

One-on-one with owner/user. Many architects begin in practices focused on one-on-one client relationships with owners or users, as in single-family custom homes. Paul Finch suggests that after the architect's design for his or her own house, where the architect covers the three roles of owner, user, and designer, "all other commissions are successive dilutions of this role."[4] In these practices, there is a direct relationship of trust between the owner/user and the designer, and there are few outside influences or stakeholders. Purpose in that perspective is implicitly to satisfy clients' lifestyle needs and create a beautiful (and safe) place.

Multiple stakeholders. Larger projects, whether institutional or corporate, almost always engage multiple stakeholders. These stakeholders often have different agendas and sometimes have competing sets of values. Often there

---

4 Finch ,Paul, preface to *Investigate ask tell draw build*, 3XN architects, London, Black Dog Publishing, 2007

are also multiple outside influences. Purpose of design in this environment is necessarily broad and performance driven, more about creating inspiring environments that are successful for the function intended and sometimes with an iconic aspiration as well. This project environment is fertile for high-performance design opportunities, but that is dependent on clients' aspirations.

Design competitions. Some practices are focused on design competitions as a primary approach to acquiring work. This is currently more common in Europe and Asia than the United States. Often these competitions either preclude or extremely limit the designer, owner, user contact until a design has been fully committed (i.e., a winning design is announced). The purpose in this approach is to win by appealing to the design jury regardless of how closely their judgment will align with the client's stated and unstated needs. Though this may change somewhat after the competition phase, it often creates quite a different sense of purpose from practices that are heavily engaged in pre-design as close client advisors and with clients playing more of a co-designer role.

Most trusted advisor/partner. Some practices focus on becoming a trusted resource for clients, and their clients' stakeholders and users (usually clients who have continuous facility needs), and in some cases with their clients' builders as well. This often creates an ethos of co-design between architect and client. The shapes of those relationships are much more intimate than one-time or sporadic-project relationships and create a very performance-centered purpose perspective. This is often the most fertile ground for high-performance design.

Form-driven versus program-driven. Another way of looking at practice experience is a contrast between those building types supposedly driven primarily by a search for iconic form (museums and corporate headquarters have often been described this way) and those buildings primarily driven by program (hospitals, laboratories, and factories have often been so described). In my view, this is a questionable way to categorize architecture, but nonetheless it has shaped some practices, sometimes with either form or program given dominance in purpose.

Hence, an architect's understanding of purpose will shape and be shaped by the nature of his or her practice experience. And the architect's understanding of purpose will determine what he or she is designing the practice to do. Where the architect defines purpose within this spectrum is less important for the creation of a high design-performance entity than the sincerity and passion for whatever the definition is.

Design for intervention in the physical world, whether it's a product or building to be used by many or a singular object to be used by few, is a commitment of the resources that make up the physical reality we all share and with which we have a mutual dependence. That inherently carries a responsibility to make such an intervention only for a positive purpose. Further, it carries a responsibility to the social contract for safety and welfare, which can be interpreted quite broadly. And, finally, it carries a contract responsibility to the client for whom we are designing. All of these add up to significant purpose even before a firm begins to consider its place in the broader arenas of purpose.

This book, however, is specifically about the quest for high-performance design. To achieve this, high performance must be central to one's purpose, whatever else it entails.

I believe that designers should feel a moral mandate to aspire and to work toward this. Designer's are as fallible as others and will not always achieve their aspirations, but I find it puzzling to try to justify lesser aspiration.

3

THE CASE FOR HIGH-PERFORMANCE DESIGN

Beyond the basic expectations of environmental enclosure and suitability for purpose, high-performance design must maximize value through high performance at reasonable cost (in time and resource).

There are many ways to assess that high value:

- **Iconic value:** formally so strong and original that it becomes a symbol for its purpose or type. Some of the best museums, such as Pei's East Building at the National Gallery or Kahn's Kimball Art Museum achieved this. SOM's Lever House did it for corporate offices.
- **Market value:** appealing so strongly and broadly that it commands a premium return in the marketplace (higher rents, higher sales price, higher occupancy, etc.)
- **Transformational value:** altering users' behavior (and culture) in a positive way, such as higher creativity, higher output, higher quality, fewer errors, higher pride, etc.
- **Cultural value:** providing a renewed or altered awareness of ethos and art.
- **Environmental Value:** providing a higher quality environment (light, air, water, view, sense of place, etc.) at less resource cost.
- **Urban value:** creating a positive experience or sense of place beyond the boundaries of itself.

High-performance design must deliver maximum value in most of these categories, and that value must be measurable in some way, not simply implied from imaginative metaphor. For most uses it should include a transformational aspect for the sponsoring enterprise.

Many owners expect that their designers will bring an indefinable something to their project that will improve their lives and enterprises. In the case of a building, it is one of the (if not the) largest single capital investments an enterprise will make to enable its activity. That indefinable something clients hope for is part of achieving high performance. That something is indefinable at the start of the process because it hasn't been discovered yet. It is the part where creativity carries reality beyond expectation.

But there are also definable expectations about what can make an enterprise better or even transformed. Those expectations can be either readily expressed by a well-prepared client or drawn out by a thorough and creative process of interactive discovery. Many of these expectations can be expressed as quantifiable goals subject to before-and-after metrics.

Further, the involvement of client and users in evoking and defining these expectations, and in the ideation and development of design, can be a large part of a process for cultural and organizational transformation for an enterprise. This is so because it brings a client face-to-face with the reality of the current situation and the possibilities of the future. If the users feel a sense of ownership of the future, then they are a good way along the path to transforming themselves. This is an important value that architecture can bring to a project.

Beyond that obligation to maximize value for clients, there are societal responsibilities made self-evident by the unsupportable rate of resource consumption and change on the planet brought about by human intervention. The self-evident aspect is that every intervention we commit as designers uses resources — renewable ones and non-renewable ones, both of which have value to society — that could be used to fulfill other equally or perhaps worthier needs. If designers do not maximize the performance produced by the use of those resources, then they have not justified their use. That inherently carries a responsibility to make our interventions as broadly positive as possible.

Design That Awakens and Inspires Human Spirit

This is the characteristic most commonly used to judge great architecture. The most recognized and honored individuals in the profession are those who regularly deliver projects that have this characteristic. It is also the aspect of design that has traditionally received the most attention in design schools. It is what motivated many of us to be designers in the first place, and in many ways it is what gives us the most creative satisfaction. If the tremendous commitment of resources we make in creating buildings, spaces, places does not raise the human spirit, what a sad loss it is to humanity. We know that it is a small fraction of the built environment that achieves this. But it is a *sine qua non* of high-performance design.

Design That Transforms the User Enterprise to a Higher Level of Performance

This is one of the key additions in expectation of high-performance design versus the usual characteristics of great architecture. Any entity undertaking a building project will be making one of its largest commitments of resources in building that project. If that entity has aspirations to become better at what it is or to become something else, then this investment provides an ideal opportunity to enable that. As customers, stock- or stakeholders, and co-habitants of the planet, we should all have such aspirations. Performance is transformed in a lot of ways that both the design process and the realized project can influence.

Design can bring people together in different ways, it can shape attitudes and self-esteem, it can shape experiences and feelings, it can help people sense things in different ways, it can reorganize flow and relationship, it can improve task conditions and teamwork conditions, it can enhance communication, it can reinforce equity and fairness, it can enhance connection to purpose. It can.

And that, too, is a *sine qua non* of high-performance design.

Design That Makes the Place (or Object) Better Than What Went Before It, Including the Context in Which It Resides

Any design displaces something that went before it, whether in physical location or mental map. If a designer is going to do that, certainly the minimum expectation must be that it will be as good as that which it displaces (does no harm). But high-performance design must improve the situation in some thoughtful way. Better clarity, connectedness, simplicity, sense of purpose or place, or healing of nature are some of the possibilities. And this extends to the context. True high performance will enhance the experience around it (e.g., create an urban event, alter perceptions in the mental map, etc.). This places an especially significant burden on design for any greenfield site and for replacement, alteration, or addition to revered landmarks.

Design That Is Accomplished with the Minimum, Essential, and Sustainable Resources

This is both a green and a fiscal commitment. The green environmental commitment has received a lot of attention lately because of increasing awareness of the negative impacts of energy and non-renewable resource use, and it is absolutely essential in high-performance design.

But in addition to the responsibility for environmental sustainability is a responsibility for all of the resources that go into project making. This is the fiscal responsibility side of the equation for high-performance design. The design and construction industry, in the United States in particular, is both one of the largest and the least efficient industries in the nation, with reasonable estimates of waste in excess of 30 percent. That kind of inefficiency is not sustainable or responsible. High-performance design must deliver its reality without waste and with as much sustainability as possible.

Design That Is Affordable to the User Enterprise and to Society

Affordability is an important issue for design. If it violates the fiscal priorities of an enterprise or, worse, cripples it or, worse yet, bankrupts it, then the design clearly has missed an important commitment. A building that may be considered great architecture yet costs so much that it becomes a symbol of excess is not high-performance design. Time is also a critical issue and goes hand-in-hand with affordability. Windows of opportunity are a reality of life. High-performance design is delivered within an affordable time frame.

Affordability to society is another important characteristic, and the criteria are much broader, including the social costs of created inequity, violation of social promise, and the environmental concerns of irreparable damage.

Taken together, these conditions create a very tough specification, one that demands pursuit across a broad spectrum of need and one that seeks both/and rather than either/or solutions. This is different than the criteria declared and/or observed in the great design honor award programs of the world because it demands great architecture, *and* performance, *and* economy of means. The last two, even if alluded to in design award programs, are almost never demanded.

In a 2009 interview on BBC's *Hard Talk*, Daniel Libeskind was asked if architecture always requires a compromise between money and art. He replied that money plays a big part but that misses the point that architecture must bring together the needs of many stakeholders in a way that makes the best overall solution, which is a form of optimization, not compromise. Bjarke Ingels says it well in his polemic *Yes Is More* : "What if trying to make everyone happy did not have to lead to compromise or the lowest common denominator? It could be a way to find the ever elusive summersault that twists and turns in order to fulfill every desire and avoid stepping on anyone's toes."[5]

Libeskind went on to say that an important part of that solution for him is that the building tells a relevant story of place, time, and culture. Every building tells a story by its very existence. Unfortunately, banal buildings have only a short story, which goes something like: I have nothing to tell you. For Libeskind, this is an essential part of that highest value in architecture.

The storytelling analogy is a good one in many ways. Some stories resonate well with our view of life and reveal things that we may not have articulated ourselves. Others may be so riddled with subplots and obscure reference that they merely confuse and frustrate.

It is the combination of storytelling — human spirit and sense awakening, matching or bettering definable (and sometimes measurable) performance expectations, developing initially indefinable creative discoveries through design, and aligning resource use with the best interests of the planet — that produces design at its highest performance value.

Competitive Survival Motivation

There is also a pure self-interest reason for Americans and for most other Western designers to pursue high-performance design. Many of these firms have enjoyed a global competitive advantage because of a perception that they are world creative leaders. But there is increasing and sometimes amazing competition from Chinese and Indian designers in the arena of form giving (and clearly in price). To remain competitive on the world stage, firms will have to deliver value well beyond form giving, and that is what high-performance design does.

All of these criteria are essential to high-performance design and collectively set a very high bar but one that is justified and achievable. It is a moral mandate for designers to pursue this.

The more that the resources we commit are used this way, the better off we will all be and the fewer total resources we will consume.

---

5 Bjarke Ingels Group, *Yes Is More* p.14,Cologne, Evergreen, 2009.

4

THE CASE FOR DESIGNING THE DESIGN FIRM

Why should a design firm have to be designed? Isn't design, like art, something that comes from the creative minds of talented designers who somehow go within themselves to discover and reveal beautiful form?

That is a reasonable question and is true to a point. It is certainly true for much of art that is its own purpose. But for design, which by definition has a purpose beyond itself, it is at best an incomplete truth. This generally applies to industrial, product, fashion, and graphic design but especially to architectural design, where every significant project has a broad and long term impact on society's interests.

Designing a design enterprise is seeking to optimize it for the purpose it is to fulfill. And since any design enterprise is driven by its people and their interactions, designing it is about optimizing those interactions to create the highest-value realized solutions consistently and efficiently.

Many great and inspiring buildings are credited to individuals as sole authors, and in a few cases that may be accurate. However, a question remains about whether any solution to an environmental intervention is the best it could have been. Seeking high-performance design is a quest for "best possible." There are many pragmatic reasons to settle for something exciting and cool but that is short of the best possible. As James L. Adams wrote: "The natural response to a problem seems to be to try to get rid of it by finding an answer — often taking the first answer that occurs and pursuing it because of one's reluctance to spend the time and mental effort needed to conjure up a richer storehouse of alternatives from which to choose."[6]

Teresa M. Amabile of Harvard University, a leader in researching and chronicling the most sustained research programs on creativity said: "The more possibilities there are to be explored and the better the strategies for exploring

[6] Adams, James L., *Conceptual Blockbusting: A Guide to Better Ideas Third Edition*, New York, Addison-Wesley Publishing, 1986, p.7.

them rapidly, the greater the likelihood of producing a novel, yet appropriate response."[7]

Except for the least complex of design problems, the best alternatives to satisfy all requirements and discover the indefinable are more likely to be brought out by a collaboration of talented (and diverse) designers who develop, analyze, and refine a significant range of possibilities than by the isolated genius of a single individual. Tom Kelley of the design firm IDEO says, "Teams are the heart of the IDEO method. It is no accident. ... Quite simply; great projects are achieved by great teams."[8]

And this seems to be true in science as well. Social scientist Brian Uzzi's work at Northwestern University analyzed a large body of published scientific papers and their frequency of peer references to conclude that "... team efforts were judged to be better and more important science than efforts by individuals."[9] Of the two major developments in physics in the early 20th century, one is mostly the work of a genius working in isolation: Albert Einstein's special and general theories of relativity (though much of the mathematics and all of the experimental evidence were by others). The second, quantum mechanics (and specifically the generally accepted Copenhagen interpretation), was the creation of a broad collaboration of diverse minds with a great deal of creative tension.

In spite of the propensity of journalists to promote the solitary genius idea, all of the most revered architects today lead teams to accomplish their work, and it is both their design talent and their ability to draw from others on their team that make their success.

Again, this is generally true of industrial, product, fashion, and graphic design, but is especially true of architectural design where the magnitude of the issues addressed is generally larger.

So if it takes a team to address these issues, can't such teams perform at the highest level simply by following a strong leader? The answer is mostly no. Teams that conform to the wishes of a genius leader can and do produce some remarkable buildings, but mostly buildings that are inspiring in form

7 Amabile, Teresa M., *Creativity in Context*, Boulder Colorado, Westview Press, 1996, p. 96.

8 Kelley, Tom, *The Art of Innovation: Lessons in Creativity from IDEO, America's Leading Design Firm* New York, Doubleday 2001, p.69.

9 Cited by Christakis, Nicholas A., and James H. Fowler in *Connected: The Surprising Power of Our Social Networks and How They Shape Our Lives*, New York, Little, Brown and Company, 2009, p.164.

rather than satisfying in the other issues of high-performance design. While occasionally in the short term this may be an effective approach, over the long haul and for complex design problems, it is grossly inefficient.

Achieving the kind of collaboration needed to find the best possible in a consistent, focused, and effective way, even in the early stages of ideation, does not happen well without thoughtful design of team and process. To focus and optimize the use of design team resources requires investigation, exploration, and ideation into what makes a team effective (i.e., a design process).

And to make it happen over the length of a project and beyond that for multiple projects over long periods, requires design of a habitat for creativity. That design must solve for all of the issues essential for success: motivation, communication, investigation, ideation, development, and execution.

Jerry Hirshberg, industrial designer and founder of Nissan Design International, said of the process: "While thinking innovatively does involve play, emotions, talent, and dreams, it also demands the fusion of these with clear-headed rationality, relentlessly hard work, and a firm, sober-eyed grasp of reality."[10]

If you accept the premise that design is for a purpose and that high-performance design is part of your purpose, then it follows that you should design the enterprise with which you intend to achieve it.

---

10 Hirshberg, Jerry, *The Creative Priority: Diving Innovative Business in the Real World*, New York, Harper Collins 1998, p. 194.

5

DESIGNING A DESIGN FIRM FOR HIGH pH

There are two things that must be done to create a high design performance firm: Unite the right people, and build the right habitat. And those two things support and reinforce each other.

I use the term "unite" about people because, for high-performance, people have to bond around a set of values, purpose, and approach to design. Within that unity, however, there must still be room for diversity (in every meaning of thee word) and room for conflict in ideas, personality, and style. Creative conflict is essential to creativity and, indeed, is what can yield the highest pH value. But it means that common values and purpose ultimately drive behaviors.

In selecting people, Robert Grudin advises: "Achievement in any profession requires a combination of logical understanding, technical skill, intuition, and pure love."[11]

Getting the right people for high performance is about finding passionate, talented people who are motivated by the challenge of an idea-rich environment in which they can contribute. These will be people who freely share ideas and contribute to the dialogue about which idea is best. They will be people who challenge those around them but share values and purpose to get to the best for the project at hand.

Uniting people for optimum creative performance is about inspiring a diverse group of people to collaborate in pursuit of a shared design vision with passion, consistently over a long period of time, and through multiple project opportunities. It is about placing the outcome of projects above personal glory and gain. It is about effectively stimulating and focusing creativity.

The design of a high-design-performance habitat is about creating the environmental conditions that enhance people's creative performance. It must deal with firm culture, approach, and structure. Each of these is interdependent and all must be focused on the purpose of design outcome.

---

[11] Grudin, Robert, *The Grace of Great Things: Creativity and Innovation* New York, Ticknor & Fields, 1990, p.184

Firm Culture

Creative performance demands an environment in which people believe in a set of shared values and the leadership of the enterprise is committed to and demonstrably lives these values. The values must embrace a sense of fairness and equity and of unbiased recognition or reward for contribution.

It also demands that there is a clearly articulated (in words, symbols, and actions) purpose for the design effort, and that purpose is both satisfying and felt to be worthy by the participants. It is valuable to have vision as well, which is an expression of aspiration for becoming something better. A vision helps focus on both the immediate importance and long-term meaning of purpose.

There must also be a sense of meaningful participation and shared authorship of the outcome. This is essential to keeping design teams engaged and interested in the success of projects through to completion, and in the success of the design enterprise over a long period.

A high pH firm's workplace will embody all of the above.

Approach

The design enterprise must have an approach or attitude about how it addresses its work that is readily understood and effective yet is also mutable through continuous learning and discovery. The approach should provide orienteering guidelines of the categories of issues to be addressed as well as a how-to experience base and examples to draw on. The application of this approach must strike an important balance between depth and breadth of discovery and ideation and effective use of time and other resources.

Even with a strong approach, the high pH design entity must have an understandable, efficient, effective process for the pursuit of design. This specifically excludes a one-size-fits-all process approach; rather, it demands a project-specific tailored process that gives adequate attention to all aspects of design essential to meaningful solution and execution. Preferably, these tailored processes are custom designed by all of the participants at the outset and throughout each stage of a design project.

To ensure that the approach and specific-project-based process stretches as far as possible in finding a high-performance design solution, the firm should regularly develop and use heuristics[12] and other effectiveness-enhancing tools. Otherwise, there is a natural tendency toward repeating what has been successful previously to the exclusion of new possibilities.

Since design is for a purpose, it is meaningless until it is fully realized, and doing that well is a critical part of the firm's approach. A key to design performance is incorporation of techniques, materials, and processes that ensure the design's success in construction and occupancy. This calls for active design collaboration with all of the parties to project implementation. And that collaboration has to happen in a sequence when it can effectively influence the design outcome.

It must also include an approach to sustaining and developing the practice itself, which deals with business model, strategy, and development.

Structure

A structure to support design activity is essential to allow design teams to focus on design. But the design of the structure and processes will only ensure performance if it is for the purpose of supporting and enhancing design, not harnessing it to a commercial or bureaucratic focused process. The structure must connect leadership with ownership of risk. It must provide logistics, facilities, and business tools in support of design.

A Word about Change

For any of this to be useful, a firm must be willing and capable of undertaking transformative change. One very helpful tool in that is John P. Kotter's work on implementing change in organizations.[13]

Kotter identifies eight key steps in successful cultural transformations. Paraphrased, these are:

- Create a sense of urgency.
- Form a powerful guiding coalition.
- Create a vision.

---

[12] Heuristic is used here to mean a tool that stimulates thinking through application of a thought rule, e.g., von Oech's thinking hats.

[13] Kotter, John P, "Leading Change: Why Transformation Efforts Fail," *Harvard Business Review*, March-April 1995, p. 59-67.

- Communicate the vision.
- Empower others to act on the vision.
- Plan to create short-term wins.
- Consolidate improvements.
- Institutionalize new approaches.

I have found his work to be particularly relevant in the design entity environment.

PEOPLE

A design firm being about people seems obvious enough, but what is it about those people that will enable an enterprise to excel in high design performance, and what will motivate them to achieve high-performance design? Passion and talent for design are certainly on the top of the list for any successful design firm, but it takes more than that to build a high pH entity.

There are essential skills in specific aspects of practice that must be covered, of course, such as research, ideation, tectonics, business, etc.

Other key characteristics are curiosity, intelligence, selflessness (or at least able to stand outside one's ego), and the ability to collaborate. To perform together, these people need to be united in passion for design, purpose, and values. How do you start to assemble or transform such a group?

Leaders/Owners

The leaders and owners of the entity must represent the qualities and values to which the practice aspires. Without this, they are not credible and will not inspire shared values.

They should either have all of the skills needed or have a sincere appreciation for them and the ability to draw them out of others. They have to demonstrate the fiery passion for design that high achievement will require.

Pick (or align) your partners well. And, by picking well, I don't mean people who will just support you. I mean people who challenge you, who will complement your skills and personality and who share your values and passion for design but see it from a different perspective. It takes a leadership group that can work together in as much creative tension as possible, short of the tension turning into time consuming dissension. Creative tension should be embraced and leveraged. It is that interaction of brilliance coming from different perspectives that leads to the best both/and solutions.

Personal tensions can be expected and must be managed. It is delightful if you can find a group that meets all of the needs for high performance and whose members' personal styles are perfect complements to each other. That is rare and precious. The alternative is to deal with interpersonal annoyances openly, focused on issues not personality and with a sense of humor. Even (or maybe especially) the most valuable team members have issues that grate on others: the credit hog (who assumes sole ownership of every team effort he or she fronts, often by the passive refusal to clarify), the blame thrower (who looks so intensely for fault that he or she rarely contributes to solutions), the tough issue groundhog (who is invisible any time a tough call has to be made), the quicker-than-light thinker (who has no patience for those with more thoughtful or circuitous processing), the out-of-context leaper (who is in so far a different place in his or her thoughts that most others can't get there without a long climb), Intense Man (whose passion scares others into submission). I am sure that you know many more. Look at the value they bring if only you have the culture to embrace them. But if personal differences are not dealt with openly, they can become devastatingly detrimental to design performance.

Diversity is essential to design performance and firm success because it provides breadth of perspective and ideas. Age, gender, ethnicity, and skill peaks are all important in diversity design.

When you have a strong leadership group, you want to keep it vibrant by enabling continuous transition. Part of every leader's responsibility should be to find and mentor (and learn from) a person who can replace and be better than that leader. That is only hard if you are insecure about yourself.

Staff

To the extent you can make it happen, you want to see similar characteristics and potential to join the leadership in all other staff you select. But you also select to create a balance of the skills necessary for the total discover, design, and deliver process. Every team needs all of the skill perspectives, and if it is to perform outstandingly it needs the highest level of each of those skills. An ideal would be that everyone was a completely rounded designer with talent, passion, and experience at the highest level in every required skill (yet with diversity in perspective). Alas, we don't develop that way, and that is what collaboration is all about. The success of a collaborating team is dependent on team composition, by design, that matches complementary skill levels so that there is a high peak skill to cover every base.

Part of that design should be to achieve what Jerry Hirshberg called "creative abrasion": "Just as the creative fusion of ideas can occur by holding seemingly antithetical thoughts in the mind simultaneously, so creative collaboration between people can occur by an effort to retain conflicting cultural and disciplinary viewpoints in the mind without discarding either."[14]

It can be very stimulating to work with brilliant people of seemingly off-the-wall perspective and internal motivation and who often have personalities that are frustratingly hard to comprehend. That effort is worth the stimulation it provides, up to the point that it becomes a serious violation of the values of the enterprise culture and therefore destructive. Managing that is a challenge, but that is what leadership is all about.

Cultural and ethnic differences can create difficulties of assimilation as well. A high pH firm must be able to see the benefit of those differences as being much more interesting than the problems.

Cultural and ethnic differences are often a challenge to culturally based values, and that is the hardest thing with which to deal. As an example, Asian cultures seem to place a significantly higher importance on personal rank or title achievement than Western cultures, certainly more than the social democracies of northern Europe, with the United States being somewhere in between. That difference in perspective, if it is not recognized, can lead to frustration and misunderstanding. If it is recognized and put on the table, it can enrich the dialogue. There are also many potential intercultural conflicts that might be encountered in a diverse staff that can catch you unawares: Armenian-Turkish, German-Polish, Chinese-Japanese, Korean-Japanese, and, maybe more recently, American-everyone else, to mention a few. If a firm is to practice globally, or even more ambitiously to establish a global practice (locally based), it must get good at both understanding and benefiting from cultural diversity.

Mergers

Mergers provide opportunity to acquire new leaders and diversity in ideas, styles, and perspectives. But mergers can be and often are disruptive to design cultures. An essential aspect of a merger for a high pH firm is cultural compatibility. There are a number of strategic reasons to do mergers, including access to great people, geography, project type, or, for growth-motivated firms, volume and market share. But, for high design performance, cultural compatibility must be a key criterion. That may be heavily tested in the pre-merger stage but must be aggressively pursued in the first year or two post-

14 Hirshberg, *op. cit.*, p. 33.

merger. In the ideal, two compatible cultures will learn from each other and become stronger through the merger, and the whole can be managed without distracting from its focus on design.

Inclusiveness

In a high pH entity, it is not just the design teams that are important, it is everyone in the firm. The design effort must be supported by creative people who also have passion for design even though they are not designers by education and may not see themselves as designers. If they respect and have passion for design, they can be motivated to use their own creativity in designing support systems and a creative environment.

Selecting people for high design performance starts with the selection of leaders or owners (who are often self-selecting) and, if you get that right, is followed by seeking everyone else as a potential leader in some way. While it is true that not all valuable people want to lead the firm, it is also true that all valuable people have the ability to lead something and to contribute to creative success.

People at NBBJ

Leadership

I will start with the effort we went through a few years after I became a partner to find alignment within the partnership. The partnership had grown rapidly for a few years as the first-generation partners handed off the firm. Four of us (self-selected) did an ad hoc redesign of the partnership to provide strategic focus. We sold that to the rest of the partners and restructured to a smaller group of five. The five in that group were all design-focused white male architects covering an age spread of about 18 years and were generally aligned in purpose around improving design performance.

Personalities at that early strategy table ranged from people/experience focused (David Hoedemaker) to relationship focused (Bill Bain) to business and planning focused (Friedl Bohm) to intellectual/analytical focus (me). That set us on the path of designing the design firm, though at first in a rather haphazard fashion. We added a few more partners based on merit and opportunity through merger over the next few years.

Gradually we shifted to adding partners much more strategically, based primarily on need and backed by merit. Need included both role-specific needs and diversity needs. Under that approach, we accomplished mergers without immediately granting partnership. That worked very well. Those joining us from mergers who proved meritorious and filled a need became partners in a reasonable length of time (e.g., Scott Wyatt, became partner, then CEO of NBBJ West, then a managing partner). We became better and much more strategic at mergers and spent a lot of effort on compatibility and inclusivity by staff exchanges, frequent face-to-face communication, and pushing joint project successes. And, when a merger didn't work out, we made every effort to undo it in a way that was positive for both sides, trying to leave the divorced firm as strong as possible.

We tried to be active rather than passive in pursuit of diversity, occasionally trying things that didn't work out and that were painful to undo. Still, I think the trials were worth it for the firm and not catastrophic for anyone.

Staff

For a long time in my early years, we had a single source of screening new hires: a very experienced, production-oriented but design-concerned partner with a strong work ethic, a high threshold for humor, and a heavy bias for conformity. A lot of people whom I have encountered over the years (and many very talented and successful designers) remember their efforts to get past that gatekeeper. It shaped their views of the firm's values in a lasting way and one that does not reflect who we like to think we have become. It is a strong reminder of the importance of the way a firm recruits.

In recent years, we recruit at a number of levels, but most design staff are recruited at the studio level, and the process is treated as a two-way street, with our staff selling what the practice has to offer and encouraging potential hires to get to know us. The potential hire is exposed to dialogue with a number of NBBJ staff focused on value passion and skill fit. That process often involves double digit encounters on many hours. In the breakfasts I have had with the successful new employees, many have commented on the value they felt they got from the rigor of that process.

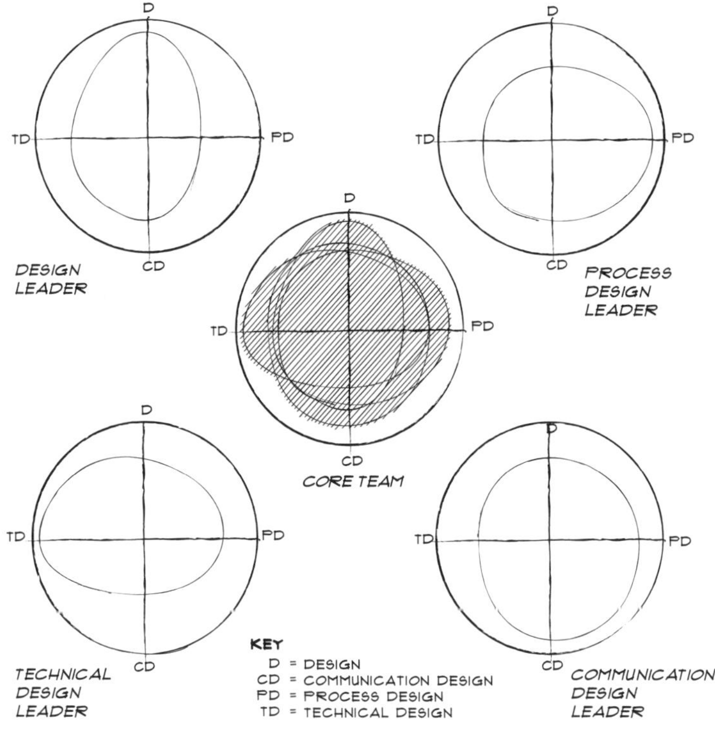

Figure 1. *Balancing core team leadership. The four outer diagrams chart the competency of each of the core team leaders. The middle is a composite showing the range of competencies covered. The point is to maximize team skill by seeing complementary peaks.*

We believe that architects need to have a strong generalist architect background to be effective design contributors. Ideally, we would like to see most of our staff with high peaks in every skill, but that is not reality. Instead, we seek a balance of people with complementary skills. We have used diagrams like those in Figure 1 to analyze balance in a studio or a team and in assessing hiring needs.

New employee intake in a firm is another important step, and that is an area where both studios and support staff need to be creative in designing affordable and effective systems. NBBJ's approach has included "sponsorship" by an associate in the studio, introduction in studio weekly meetings, orientation by HR and IT staff, and of course the breakfasts with managing partners mentioned elsewhere.

In the 1970s, before we had our current emphasis on a performance culture and in spite of the gatekeeper I described above, we had a lead designer who fit all of the criteria of the "brilliant people of seemingly off-the-wall perspective." He was highly creative and helped us win a couple of important design competitions that resulted in important commissions. His behavior was bizarre and, for a while, amusing. He was challenging and stimulating across a spectrum of domains from science to psychology. He tested me often with questions about quantum mechanics versus relativity, and Jung versus Freud. I couldn't always comprehend his questions, which were variously stimulating, amusing, and annoying. He was an early headphone adopter and often worked only outside of normal business hours. He grew more and more cynical and bizarre as time went by. When he left the firm, his bizarre behavior continued with cryptic and puzzling postcards (from hell, thought some recipients). You may well recognize the personality from your own experience. The projects, though good enough to win competitions, were not our best work even at that time.

Was it worth it to NBBJ? I think it was at the time because he represented an edge that we needed to get much closer to, and having an extreme example made taking risk on things short of that seem safer. We would not benefit from that today, both because we don't need to be taught the value of the edge and because we know that delivering high-performance design requires collaboration start to finish.

In the 1990s, when we were well into the quest for high design performance, we had opportunities to bring a few well established designers into the firm. This is always a challenge to a culture's immune system. The issue is whether a person with a well entrenched cultural outlook can be assimilated and embraced, or will be rejected or cause fracturing. And based on risk analysis, is it worth trying?

We tried several, and all produced some benefit to our quest.

One of the most beneficial is Peter Pran. Peter had a reputation that was well established by published work but with only a few built projects done while he was with Ellerbe. Though he had a number of fans and supporters, bringing him into the firm was very controversial internally, and we had a lot of heated dialogue around the issue among leaders in the firm. I had a conviction that what he brought was right for what we needed at that time, and I used a lot of my forceful personality (Marilyn, my wife, says that is outrageous hyperbole) to win acceptance of the idea. And like most designers who matured their careers in other environments, our culture was a struggle for Peter. And it was difficult for some of us to work with him. But his passion for design outcome and the passion and curiosity of our culture made it work. We had a mutual impact on each other's approach: Peter pushed us on possibility of form, and we pushed Peter on design content and relevance. He has led and continues to lead design teams on a number of very strong projects for us. Just as important as his direct influence has been the other designers who have followed him to NBBJ. Two of our partners — Tim Johnson and Jonathan Ward — are at the top of that impressive list.

We experienced firsthand the problems created by unacknowledged cultural differences, and in spite of putting a lot of energy into it, we were not able to salvage a few relationships and lost some very talented people because of it. But we continue to work at this because we know the benefits of this diversity to the creative process, and because we are practicing globally, establishing a locally based global practice in London and Shanghai.

In Shanghai, we benefitted greatly from the leadership of a Shanghai-raised Chinese citizen, Jerry Yin, who did post-graduate study in the United States and joined our practice in Seattle. Jerry was with us for about 10 years in the United States, and he led design teams on several award-winning projects here. At the same time, he helped us break into markets in Shanghai. He became a principal in the firm and moved his family back to China to found and build our Shanghai office.

A long-time-in-coming lesson learned was that the more rigorous our project focus and approach, the easier it was both to accommodate and benefit from diversity in people's perspective, skills, and personalities.

As of this writing, NBBJ has — 37 nationalities represented on its staff, is 42 percent female, and 25 percent minority. Partner age spans 27 years, and three of 15 are women.

People in Danish Design Firms[15]

The Danish design firms I include in this review are all widely published and honored, have won a number of design awards, and have projects that I think approach or encompass the criteria for high-performance design. I chose them because of this.

Unsurprisingly, the large majority of staff in the firms I investigated are Scandinavians and mostly Danes. Though there is diversity in these firms, the Danish ethos dominates the staff. There is an inherent advantage in this in several ways: the Danes have an egalitarian attitude[16] that is inherently collaborative (egos are generally in check), there is a societal appreciation if not reverence for design and distrust of excess, and most of the Danes come from one of two design schools, so they start with a reasonably aligned view of design purpose.

The opposite side of that coin, of course, is that that homogeneity can limit perspective. Bjarke Ingels describes the downside as creating "a grey goo of sameness" with "all libido invested in polishing and perfecting the ever finer details. The sum of all the little concerns seems to have blocked the view of the big picture."[17] All of these firms have made efforts to seek more diversity, adding non-Scandinavians to their staffs and stretching beyond architects.

3XN went from an initial three partners down to one founding partner, who has since selected four more to join him. The partners are all architects, though one focuses on management, and they cover an age span of about 15 years. With a staff of 100, the firm is about 10 percent non-Scandinavian and has added disciplinary diversity by creating a technology research arm called GXN.

Arkitema, founded in 1969-1970 by five architecture students from Aarhus with, according to them, "very different personalities, but an awareness of each other's strengths and weaknesses gives them precisely the kind of dynamics that have subsequently characterized the practice." They added partners in 1995 and 2002 and

[15] For a brief description of these firms, see the Notes at the end of this book.

[16] This comes from a number of historic influences. One is an attitude toward individuality and success common in Scandinavia known as Jante Law, essentially "Don't think that you are better than anyone else." The term originated in the 1933 novel *A Fugitive Crosses His Tracks,* by Aksel Sandermose. A second is the widespread teachings of 19th-century pastor, author, and educator N.F.S. Grundtvig, who was the ideological father of the Danish folk high schools and advocated creativity, compassion, cooperation, and equality. And a third was the development of the Danish welfare state largely under the authorship of Thorvald Stauning, social democratic prime minister twice between 1924 and 1942. Naturally, this ethos is morphing with younger generations and this uniformity may be eroding.

[17] Bjarke Ingels Group, *op. cit.*, p. 14.

are now at a total of 13, with all of the founders scheduled to retire as a group in 2010. That is a remarkable event for a design practice and a unique approach to transition. With a total staff of about 160, they have Chinese architects as well as a number of non-architectural disciplines (landscape architects, construction managers, economists, artists, and graphic designers).

BIG currently has six partners and two associate partners, one of whom is a woman managing director. The partners seem picked to complement Bjarke Ingels. Founded in about 2002, this is the youngest and may be the most diverse of these firms by percentage of staff, with about 40 percent of its staff of 80 being non-Scandinavian. This firm also has a high percentage of intern architects.

C.F. Moller, the longest established of these firms, has a total staff of more than 300, two-thirds of whom are Danes and about 15 percent of whom are non-Scandinavian. Sixteen different nationalities are represented, likely making them the most diverse of these firms by nationality. Their staff includes industrial designers, landscape architects, engineers, and other discipline consultants, such as economists and health care professionals. They are 45 percent women, and two of their nine partners are women. One partner is Italian born and one is German born. They are a third-generation firm, diverse in age and presumably chose each other in joining this partnership.

Henning Larsen has a staff of 130, about 6 percent to 8 percent of whom are non-Scandinavians. Thirty-four percent are women. One of the six partners, all architects, is a woman, Mette Kinne Frandsen, who is also CEO. There are eight associate partners, also all architects, two of whom are women. This is a second-generation firm, with the founding partner just recently turning over majority ownership. Three of the partners form the management team, with two design directors Peer Teglgaard Jeppeson (Scandinavian projects) and Louis Becker (International projects) joining Frandsen.

Schmidt Hammer Lassen was founded by the namesakes in 1986. They have since added two partners and three associate partners, one of whom is a woman. They have a female accountant CEO. The staff is now about 140. Approximately 15 percent are women, and 5 percent are non-Scandinavians.

The people diversity in these firms seems very similar to what one would find in a comparable selection of North American firms. Yet they seem to have an underlying unity of values that is remarkable. I believe that set of underlying values allows them to readily focus on design projects with a consensus on purpose.

HABITAT

The right people are essential to achieving high-performance design, but if those people do not interact in a creativity-enhancing and efficient way, the outcome will not be that. A collection of great people who are not motivated, structured, and led in a way that allows them to build off each other's strengths can lead to worse, not better, outcomes.

The importance of habitat is that it shapes the interaction of people. Design happens because of creative people, but the way that it happens and the likelihood for high-performance outcomes is shaped by the habitat in which it takes place. Highly creative people can perform badly in an ineffective, or worse, a destructive habitat. Habitat can encourage mutual trust and respect, collaboration, focus, purpose, values, efficiency, confidence, curiosity, courage, fairness, and accountability — or it can it can encourage the opposite.

Firm habitat includes culture, approach, and structure. Each of these has a profound impact on the way a design team performs. Each of these interrelates with the others and all must be designed with design performance as their purpose. Of the three, culture is the most difficult to design because it is the result of human factors that can be heavily influenced but not directly determined, such as individual interpretation and reaction to firm actions. The design and building of this habitat is a continuous process constantly responding to new learning (and avoiding flavor-of-the-month fashions).

To get to the point of having a cohesive performance habitat that a majority of staff recognize and can articulate takes a while. It is trust-based and established by actions. Words are important to explain intent but by themselves do not establish attitude and belief. Modifying an established habitat is likely to take one or two years before a significant transformative effect is seen.

Starting from scratch takes less time to create cohesiveness, but the habitat will not really be tested until the firm is regularly doing significant multi-stakeholder work, and that is not likely until it is well beyond a startup scale.

In describing what I believe is essential to designing a high pH design practice, I use "must" and "has to" a lot, referring to what the firm design should accomplish. I do this because I believe that all of these are a part of an interrelated whole that creates internal consistency and integrity that are critical to reducing drag on focused creativity critical to design performance. I don't tell you how you "must" do it, but I suggest things that have worked in my experience and encourage the reader to be creative in addressing the issues.

Habitat at NBBJ

We came at this issue in a very roundabout way, trying to improve by structural means and discovering the interconnectedness with culture and even later learning to deal in a serious way with approach. The process was a continual series of steps of discovery with one successful trial leading to more questions, often in a seemingly unrelated area, leading to design of more trials, leading to some successes, leading to more questions. Yes, it has been a somewhat Darwinian quest.

Habitat at Danish Firms

Of these six firms, Arkitema is the only one whose leaders articulate an attitude about their habitat, saying they "focus very much on the environment in which the staff member operates." As you will see in what follows, all of the firms have established a creative environment. Both the underlying societal values and certain social norms of the country, such as lunching together (provided by the firms) and shared (nationally mandated) educational experiences, help create a habitat that has many of the attributes I think are essential to high-performance design.

CULTURE

Values, Purpose, Participation, Communication

A firm's culture is what demonstrates its true brand ... what the firm stands for. Although the leadership of a firm influences and shapes the culture, this is one key aspect of high pH that leadership cannot directly design or create. It is created by the people in it based on their behaviors (which are in response to leaders' actions, among other things). Their behavior comes from what they believe and the values they share. Culture is critical to performance because it infects the behavior and performance of everyone who joins the firm. Every person new to a firm is ultimately informed by its culture more than anything else. Staff's perception of the culture determines how people fit in, how they are motivated, and what they think is acceptable behavior.

Teresa Amabile's research has led her to believe that "Work environments most conducive to fulfillment of creative potential may include: a high level of worker responsibility for initiating new activities, a low level of interference from administrative superiors, and a high stability of employment."[18] All of these are worthy cultural goals for high design performance.

For leaders to have the influence they desire on shaping a culture, they must have a sincere commitment to the set of values and purpose they espouse. They must communicate those values and purpose articulately, consistently, continuously, and frequently. And most important, they must live those values and purpose conspicuously and reliably. For many designers this is a tiresome burden they were not trained for and that they see as a distraction from what they think of as design. They are wrong, if their purpose is to create high-performance designs.

Most creative people (those who will perform well in a high-performance practice) are sensitive to the cultures they engage and are attracted or repelled by what a culture tells them. A strong culture focused on achieving high performance will be a magnet to those who cherish that challenge and an immune system repelling those who are not motivated by it.

Culture is in some ways intangible, but it can be very tangible to an outsider.

[18] Amabile, *opus cit.*, p.229.

When someone makes a personal visit to a design firm for the first time he or she is struck by impressions of the culture manifested by the buzz, or lack of it, around the work and by the attitude of excitement, curiosity, responsibility, and joy of engagement, or of course the lack of any of these. And certainly people respond to the presence or lack of physical manifestation of design in the place. These manifestations of culture are apparent to visiting clients. During the process of designer selection the sense of cultural compatibility can be an influential factor to any discerning client, and that certainly means those seeking a high-performance design.

Culture is the sum of what a firm is. It is the reflection of values, purpose, aspirations, and attitudes as they are lived. It reflects reality, not rhetoric. It is something that can be influenced and enabled, but it cannot be directly designed. It will be created by human response to how everything else in the firm's design is realized and lived. It is one of the two most important metrics of a firm's success, the other being the work itself. This is a reality in designing the design firm. As a leader, you can design much of the practice, and that will help shape the culture, and your leadership will help shape it. But the culture will be a result of all those factors and the people in the culture. If you have done well with the people side, and all of the other aspects of habitat, then the culture will perform and most likely have a very interesting personality.

Culture at NBBJ

NBBJ in the mid 1960s was a largish practice (60 to 70 people) with a slight tilt toward a business focus. There were designers both inside and outside the firm who were critical of our design purpose. Though we were successful in getting excellent design opportunities, the firm culture was not focused on high performance.

We became aware of the importance of our culture to our design success through a process of trying to change design-related-aspects of the practice and discovering how interrelated everything is. We came to realize that we must examine how people behave to know what our real culture is. There are many things that can be done to help shape what your culture becomes, but at any point in time what the culture really is is demonstrated by how the firm behaves. How firm leadership and staff deal with a significant firm crisis (workload, personal tragedy, whatever) will often do the most to shape and reveal cultural attitudes and belief, and that was true for us.

Culture in Danish Firms

All the firms I reviewed appeared to have an essentially egalitarian culture in which open dialogue was the norm. Two (C.F.Moller and Schmidt Hammer Lassen) talked about a social democratic ethic in describing how they work, and Arkitema talks about "respect for the individual and for the non-hierarchical aspects of our culture and our approach." All six firms have an apparent and, in most cases, articulated sense of social responsibility and focus on design. All work in essentially open plan environments.

VALUES

Honesty and Humanity; Curiosity, Risk and Safe Failure; Shared Responsibility and Collaboration

Design requires a passionate involvement and commitment to bring out creative solutions to complex issues. People are motivated to make this commitment only if they feel that the result will be worthwhile, and specifically that it will embody the human values in which they believe. It is critical for long-term success that the leaders of a design practice are articulate, sincere, and forthcoming in revealing the values they share in the practice. The willingness of others to work within these values will depend on the degree of alignment between the firm's and their own values. But a lack of clarity or insincerity about a firm's values from its leaders almost always leads to dissension and disappointment in the firm.

The values that a practice has should be the least mutable aspect of a firm, yet even these values can change over time as the needs of society change or are revealed in different ways. Sustainability, for instance, while seen as an important value by many people for a long time, became both more compelling and more urgent with the revelation of links to global warming and an understanding of that impact.

There are a lot of ways to communicate values, and using a number of them is essential to imbed them in a culture. Clearly the most important communication of values is for the leaders to live them visibly and consistently. But direct articulation is also essential. One of the most effective and long-lasting examples I am aware of is Sir Ove Arup's *The Key Speech*[19] to his firm in 1970, a tract that has come to have iconic value and the impact of which has lasted more than 40 years.

Annual or semi-annual reiteration of values as part of state-of-the-firm messages, whether in speech, video presentation, or written, are essential. Inscribing a value statement into workplace architecture can also be useful and suggests the minimal amount of mutability that values should have. But it is living those values consistently that makes them real.

---

[19] Sir Ove Arup, *The Key Speech*, delivered July 9, 1970, to his partners at a meeting in Winchester, England, available on the Arup Web site *www.arup.com.*

Honesty and humanity go hand-in-hand if they are to have a positive effect on people in design. Honesty is critical to meaningful exploration and evaluation of ideas. Yet if honesty is not expressed in terms of an empathetic humanity, it can easily become personal and destructive. A high-performance culture must focus on issues, not on personalities. People who have difficulty critiquing design in a non-personal way must be coached and learn by example. If that doesn't happen, honesty cannot flourish.

Honesty and humanity must also permeate the financial approach of a successful design enterprise both internally and externally. A compensation approach that is transparently fair and reasonably related to the enterprise's own prosperity (in good times and bad) is essential to keep that aspect of practice from being a distraction and a drag on the exciting work of design. A business approach that transparently maintains respect for the value delivered and has empathy for the customers' perspective is also key to success. There are important lessons to be learned from the effects of the distortion of values and honesty in financial firms that precipitated the 2008 world financial crisis.

Curiosity will endure and permeate a culture only if it is nurtured, encouraged, rewarded, and demonstrated by leadership. The importance of curiosity is that it enables thinking beyond the stereotype and encourages an understanding of underlying causality in existing as well as potential relationships.

At Toyota, process improvement curiosity enables penetration through the five "whys" to discover a true root cause. When a question is allowed to be called "dumb," curiosity is immediately retarded. Curiosity must exist for all aspects of design, from what a client perceives as success and why, to what society needs from a specific project or project site, and why. The realm of ideation is expanded by a wide base of knowledge and experience gained through persistent curiosity.

Curiosity can be nurtured and learned if people see that this quality is valued. Only by being aggressively curious and open to all ideas that reveal themselves will the most relevant solutions unfold. And only if all team members share that curiosity will the richest array of possibilities be revealed.

Risk and safe failure is a key concept for performance. Taking risk must be encouraged if creative breakthroughs are to happen. It is an important attitude that empowers pushing the envelope of creativity. Tom Kelley says about his firm: "We've got a saying around IDEO: 'Fail often to succeed sooner.'"[20]

The role of leaders in a high design performance enterprise is to provide the encouragement to take risk and the guardrails to ensure that no failure is catastrophic to anyone (client, society, individual, team, studio, or design enterprise). The leader's role is also to draw the benefits from failure in both learning and potential future use of temporarily failed ideas.

One obvious area to deal with is losses that are experienced in design competitions. A lost competition is particularly hard on younger team members. A leader's job is to make the loss a learning experience and to make apparent the benefits of having competed in spite of the loss. Competitions can draw a team together, heighten their creative skills, and lay a groundwork of great ideas that can be called upon in other work. In another chapter, I describe how a series of competitions at NBBJ led to development of a new building typology.

A tougher issue is when someone hasn't worked well in a specific role and a change must be made. If the culture is one that treats all roles as temporal and non-tenured and establishes a history of dignified succession from one role to another, this is not difficult. A flat or non-hierarchical environment makes this much easier because it greatly reduces the demoting feel of some transitions, which can be demoralizing, de-motivating, and occasionally in the words of the great Daffy Duck, "deee-spicable." This environment also encourages self-awareness of suitability for roles and yields helpful voluntary changes when roles are not working.

An ethic of shared responsibility for outcome is the ultimate result of true collaboration where everyone feels a sense of contribution. It is an outcome of leaders who address problems as issues to solve and do not use blame as a solution. It is achieved by everyone buying into and understanding goals and metrics of success. When that exists, problems and potential problems get identified and articulated early and solutions are found in a timely way. The Toyota approach of stopping an assembly line to focus on a problem is an example of this kind of mentality. Inherent in this ethic is accountability for the outcome and to each other. As Dr. Atul Gawande states it, "'That's not my problem' is possibly the worst thing people can think, whether they are starting an operation, taxiing an airplane full of passengers down a runway, or building a thousand-foot-tall skyscraper."[21]

20 Kelley, Tom, *op. cit.*, p. 232.

21 Gawande, Atul, *The Checklist Manifesto: How to Get Things Right*, New York, Metropolitan Books, 2009, p. 103.

An ethic of shared responsibility replaces the troublesome notion of "They did this" (and the failure to raise and solve issues enabled by that mind set) with "This is ours, and we need to make it right."

Collaboration is essential to high-performance design, but it is an art that is much harder to practice than many imagine. Team projects are included in most design school curricula, but that tends to be a weak version of what collaboration really requires, which is for people with a wide diversity of perspective, education, and skill to contribute openly to design exploration, analysis, and execution. This requires the ability for strongly design-oriented individuals to keep their ego in check and for team leaders to draw out some people more than they are comfortable being drawn out. It also requires managing an exploratory process in an objectively curious but time-effective way. These skills are rarely if ever honed during the educational process.

Also, there may be a natural tendency for designers to seek sole authorship of their own vision. That is a significant hindrance to collaboration. For true collaboration to take place, there must be trust that others working on the project have something to contribute and interest in learning what that is as well as building on it. This requires leadership skill in drawing out all participants in a way that allows them to share their ideas while not losing those whose natural style of dominance and impatience might disengage them through boredom with the process.

Collaboration can only work in an environment of mutual respect, which means not only respect for each other's talents but also for different perspectives and styles of communication. This is a skill that can be learned, but it has to be based on a belief in collaboration's benefits. Until a designer has experienced the intensity and productivity of a great collaboration, that belief is hard to come by. Leaders have an important job to demonstrate these benefits early to newcomers to design collaboration.

Collaboration is also about selecting the parties essential to the success of the project and designing the process to include them effectively. This cuts across a lot of disciplines and goes against a lot of entrenched habits such as:

- Interior designers as late-entry "rag pickers"
- Landscape architects who need only be there in time to foliate

- Planners who can be dismissed when the entitlements package is approved
- Engineers (particularly mechanical and electrical) who don't want to contribute creatively until the architectural concept is frozen
- Builders or production engineers who needn't be engaged until real cost data is required

The point is that solving design issues to maximize performance for complex enterprises requires a collaboration that engages all of the disciplines affecting the project outcome and engages them at a time and in a way that allows their creativity to benefit the outcome.

This is difficult to do effectively and requires a culture that not only supports that behavior but insists on it. Collaboration does not mean consensus decision making, though in great team experiences it can feel that way. Great collaboration is leadership-intensive in guiding the process and in decision making.

Values at NBBJ

NBBJ's values were clear in the founding partners and were well demonstrated by Perry Johanson (1910-1981), the last practicing founding partner. Perry was a great listener and a thoughtful speaker. He was self-effacing, empathetic, scrupulously honest, and passionate for architecture and for what he felt was right. He was a strong influence on my generation of partners. We hope that for the most part we have continued to live those values and that they have been implicit in our actions.

Values are reflected in the firm's vision for becoming and its purpose for being. A few years ago, we managing partners decided that it would be worthwhile to articulate values more specifically and shared the following with the firm at annual state-of-firm dialogues and in written form:

Honest and ethical behavior is our highest value.

We are here for our work. Clients and projects are the top of our pyramid.

None of us is as smart or as important as all of us. Empowered people working collaboratively is the NBBJ way.

The firm is our people.

- We are a role-based, leadership-intensive practice.
- We are optimistic and we are responsible.
- We expect everyone to be a lifelong learner and teacher.
- Our work? Design excellence — delivered and sustained.

Though this seemed to be well received at the time, I am not sure that it is particularly enlightening, and parts of it seem to me to be off the mark and a lot less passionate than I hope our actions demonstrate. If it were expressed today, it would likely be more specific about accountability. It did not generate the challenging dialogue that our vision, purpose, and brand discussions have, but maybe it will at some point.

In 2005, after I had announced my desire to phase down and a four-year plan had been put in place, my partners asked me to leave them with some thoughts about the firm. As a result, I gave them a paper on how we were building a legacy. It has some interesting observations but also will give some insight into how we dealt with values. It is included in the notes at the end of the book titled *Values in a Design Practice: 40 Years at NBBJ.*

Honesty and Humanity

As we got rigorous about the design of our practice at NBBJ, we realized that honesty is essential for the design process. If we were going to look at our work and our processes objectively, we needed to be honest with ourselves and make it safe for staff to be honest about what they saw and felt. To do that, honesty and integrity had to be manifest in all aspects of the practice.

In the economic downturn of the early 1980s, we were struggling with poor financial performance and significant layoffs, a time that can tip morale into the Dumpster. We used it as an opportunity to open up to the entire staff, seeking their help, and developing buy-in on a strategy for dealing with the problem. As part of that, we began openly sharing financial and compensation information, which had never been done before. This had to go hand-in-hand with a lot of education about the economic model and how everything influenced it, down to the level of the individual. We spent a lot of time during this period in dialogue with individuals, teams, studios, and leaders in every format and venue imaginable.

Fortunately, CFO Cece Haw, who helped develop the strategy and presentation, was a young, smart, enthusiastic cheerleader for design outcome. This was transformative in many ways, created a broad base of genuine trust and became a great foundation for the ethic of joint responsibility for outcome. It also educated staff to understand the business side of design and enable them to contribute their creative thinking to future improvement.

An important aspect of the strategy at that time was for the partners to lead in taking a very significant but temporary salary reduction and asking other titled staff to take progressively smaller temporary reductions to maintain as much stability for the staff as reasonable. We recovered in about eight months, and this approach, reached collaboratively, was a clear statement of values consistent with Amabile's idea that stability is an important condition for creativity.

At the same time, we were struggling to create an open constructive design critique environment.

Curiosity

We tried to foster curiosity at NBBJ in a number of ways. There were often discussions about books and concepts from science (e.g., chaos theory and phase change materials) as well as social economics (e.g., Daniel Pink's *A Whole New Mind,* Jeffrey Sachs' *The End of Poverty*). We brought in a number of authors for lectures and discussions, including John Medina, author of *Brain Rules*; Roger Martin, author of *The Opposable Mind* and *The Design of Business*; and Richard Swett, author of *Leadership by Design.*

One approach that is effective is an annual exploratory event, largely for younger staff, called Oregano (after the spice). Every studio nominates one or two candidates for a group trip to explore some part of the world together for a couple of weeks. The trips are organized by two principal design leaders, paid for by the firm, and include visits to design firms and cultural events in addition to time for individual exploration. Following their return, these groups host a culturally representative information-sharing party for each office in addition to making individual experience-sharing presentations.

We encouraged self-initiated exploration of issues of interest. Out of that environment came many interesting and useful things. An ad hoc group calling themselves the Merry Pranksters put forth a series of ideas about firm organization that identified unacknowledged elephants in the room and potential ways of dealing with them. Before long that led to one of our many adjustments in structure. A bright young architect, Blaine Brownell, began exploring new materials and systems, not necessarily intended for buildings, and putting them out in a product-of-the-week blog. This grew to an incredibly interesting catalog and a book *Transmaterial: A Catalog of Materials That Redefine Our Physical Environment.*[22] When I have referenced this in my teaching role at the University of Hawaii, many students were already aware of it and had been influenced by it. I have also been surprised by how many architects I have encountered around the world, including one of the Danish firms described in this book, that have been aware of it. It was a great internal resource for NBBJ and a helpful indicator of the firm's support for curiosity.

Risk and Failure

We dealt with transition at the leadership level in an aggressively motivating way, starting with the five-year reorganization of the partnership in the late 1970s, when we went from a partnership of 21 to a partnership of five with 15 non-part-

[22] Brownell, Blaine, ed., New York, Princeton Architectural Press, 2004.

ner principals (only one left the firm). This transition was made to focus strategy decisions. We did not change anyone's primary role, all principals still had a share of profits, and partners (though they held the equity and the liability) had "principal" on their business cards.

We changed the CEO position a number of times as conditions changed and the role demanded different skills. When we did that we generally changed the role definition and made the change positive for the people transitioning out of the role by placing them in another important role needing their skills. A couple of these transitions were initiated by the CEO himself, who felt that at that time the firm needed a change or a skill that wasn't his strength.

When we tried mergers or new service entities, we generally set an expectation that we would make them work within three years. If not, we would abort, unless there was an extraordinary reason not to. The implicit acknowledgement was that these are risky ventures that don't always work out, and everyone's job was to give it their best shot but not to be crushed if it didn't work. We sometimes extended that expectation if we had not reached a target but saw alternative approaches to try, and the goal was critical enough. When we did that, the reasons for it had to be openly explained, and had to make sense or it caused a lot of concern about the rigor of our commitments. Every breach of trust takes many, many kept commitments to even the balance.

Shared Responsibility

We were emphatic that everyone touching a project has responsibility for its total outcome regardless of his or her specific role on the project. And total project outcome means design quality, transformational quality, process and economic success, and project realization/implementation. On one large medical center project, the lead design principal did the detail drawings for all of the toilet rooms, both balancing team workload and, as it turned out, creating what became an iconic demonstration of the attitude that everyone has responsibility for the outcome.

Later, we were impressed with Rosamund and Benjamin Zander's notion of the value of "leading from any chair"[23] and used the term to push responsibility for leadership of each aspect of our work to the person who most directly influenced it.

---

23 Zander, Rosamund Stone, and Benjamin Zander, *The Art of Possibility*, New York: Penguin Books 2002, p. 73.

The leadership of our project teams, our studios, and the firm are all in the hands of what we call core teams. These are teams in which each person has a specific role of advocacy and competency, but everyone is jointly responsible for the outcome regardless of specific role. A typical project core team includes a design leader, process designer, and technical designer. With everyone feeling responsibility for the outcome, they are focused on helping wherever there is a need and holding each other accountable — not for sake of blame (one of the cancers in any creative endeavor) but for solution seeking. Holding people accountable extends to the leaders and owners of the firm, and new employees are encouraged to do that in their early breakfast with managing partners. Many of them have found it safe enough to do just that, much to our benefit.

Recently, the firm has added an expectation that all projects will set up a peer review process to increase emphasis on accountability. This usually (but not always) is internal to the firm but external to the studio. External peer review of selected work is also done annually.

Collaboration

When I joined NBBJ in the mid 1960s, the firm had just spun off its interior design staff into a wholly owned separate entity (called Business Space Design) for two reasons. One was the perceived market advantage of an entity that could pursue tenant fit out work independent of the architecture practice, but the other was to gain better respect for and therefore collaboration with interior design talent who had been treated as supportive second citizens. This was a very familiar story between architects and (particularly "captive") interior designers at the time.

We later did a similar thing with cost estimating (an entity called Project Cost Management), management consulting and urban planning (an entity called Management & Planning Services), and retail planning (Retail Concepts). At the time, these had a benefit of improving morale for the staff of those entities and caused working relationships with NBBJ architects to become mutually more satisfying and respectful.

By the late 1980s, however, as NBBJ created a better habitat for collaboration enhanced by what it was learning from the recent change to a studio-based culture, those arm's-length relationships began to get in the way. We gradually reintegrated those entities, and close collaboration based on mutual respect gradually became a new norm (or close to it).

At NBBJ, as at most design firms, overcoming natural barriers to true collaboration is an issue that requires continuous attention and a lot of patience. Most of us are no more aware of the limitations we put on collaboration than we are of our social biases and bigotry, and to address that is painful at times. Many of us have had experiences designing with others in which we felt we were collaborating by listening to their points of view before we decided what to do. It took a long time to get to understand what the issues and benefits of real collaboration are. Real collaboration engages people with a wide diversity of perspective, education, and skill to contribute openly to design exploration, analysis, and execution for the benefit of a more brilliant and broadly based solution. Generally, collaboration is learned in different layers at different times. For instance, dealing with a strong and imaginative structural design firm (in our case John Skilling, Jack Christiansen and now John Magnusen, Ron Klemensic of the firm that now bears the latter two names), it was easy to get to a rich collaboration both because the enthusiastic creativity was there and because it was in a realm that clearly did not compete with our own sense of role. It is much harder to get past feeling competitive with those of similar backgrounds who are focused on basically the same issues. And beyond the core architecture project team, we have to overcome stereotypes of roles we have assumed for interior designers (rag pickers), landscape architects (plant guys), etc. And of course, it continues as we expand our thinking about how to get to effectively delivered design and want to include builders and fabricators. We have had to teach ourselves how to relate effectively to other personalities, perspectives, and communication styles. This has meant becoming patient teachers and sincere learners as we bring them into a design process that is likely foreign to their experience.

The good thing is that you get better with practice, and with practice you encounter the rich reward in better design that this can bring. NBBJ achieved most of its high-performance designs when it was collaborating at its best. That was true of our projects included in this book and of other high-performance design projects of ours such as the Banner Health hospitals in Arizona, the U.S Federal Courthouse in Seattle, and the Cal IT 2 laboratory at UC San Diego.

I personally have had opportunities to collaborate with a number of other architects — most, but not all, successfully. Two were great learning experiences in collaborative style.

I led a team working on an invited design competition for a new town on the coast in the southern end of the Korean peninsula. Aldo Giurgula and his partner Hal Guida were on the team, and I had four designers from NBBJ with me. We held a charrette on site for several days, during the course of which we evolved concepts both by parallel small teams and by group critique and ideation. Aldo was the most venerated designer on the team, but his style of collaboration was amazing. After each group gathering for a pin-up and critique of our several schemes, we would take a coffee break, and Aldo would redraw every scheme in his wonderful semi-abstract, essence-only style, incorporating comment from the critique and totally leveling the playing field in terms of presentation. We would then discuss the schemes in this new and seemingly very objective light before moving on. Everyone was energized by this, and in the end everyone felt complete ownership of the final design.

The other memorable learning experience was working with Renzo Piano on a competition for a medical center replacement at NIH in Bethesda. Rich Dallam, Charles Martin, and I stayed in Genoa to work on this in Piano's studio with him and a couple of his principals. He has a large round table at the lowest level of his hillside greenhouse-like studio. We all sat around that table discussing and making napkin sketches of concepts as we talked. Piano would draw out each of us on the ideas suggested, often modifying a sketch as we talked. Standing over his shoulder was an elderly woodworking craftsman. Frequently, Piano would hand him a sketch and he would scurry over to the wood shop directly behind the table. The dialogue would continue (over the only slightly muffled sound of saws, routers, and sanders), and the craftsman would return an amazingly few minutes later with a stunning hardwood concept model based on the last sketch. This would then be used to enrich and add a three-dimensional, tactile, and olfactory experience to the dialogue. In an afternoon we would fill the table to overflowing with beautiful models that told us a lot about the implications of each design direction and made everyone feel an intimate involvement in their development.

As a footnote, our team lost to Bob Frasca's ZGF team on which NBBJ was an associate architect for health care planning, a totally separate NBBJ studio team. This was a "Chinese Wall" team separation that was genuine. Only in reading about the Wall Street collapse did I realize how that concept became a joke in supposedly separate arms of investment firms. Yet it was real among design firms.

Values in Danish Firms

There is an inherently uniform ethos underlying Danish design firms largely for the reasons I brought out in this chapter's People section: a design-conscious country, social democratic values, egalitarian society, and common educational experience. This is the starting point of values in all of these firms.

3XN does not have a statement of values, but the firm began with an attitude of "defiance of the anti-humanistic modernism," and one would draw from their approach to work that their values center on people and place.

Arkitema does not have a statement of values, but "people in architecture" heads their description of themselves, and they articulate belief in sustainability, user involvement, and technology as a means to effectiveness. They believe in evidence-based design. Though these are not articulated specifically as values, they clearly are and they are clear to those in the firm.

BIG's values seem broadly expressed as making great things happen in the real world by taking seeming conflicts as opportunities to create new solutions. These are not encapsulated in a value statement.

C.F.Moller is perhaps the most thoughtful of these firms about values, reflecting the maturity of the practice. In addition to ideals of "simplicity, clarity, and unpretentiousness," they articulate that "C.F. Moller Architects' fundamental business values are independence, credibility, and professionalism." Each of these is further explained and tied to their behavior as a firm. They have written policies on sustainability and responsibility and a 15-point policy on environmental services and their operations. They include "the importance of harmonizing work and family and recognize the social responsibility of practice." They are affiliated with the United Nations Global Compact on human rights, labor, environment protection, and anti-corruption.

And here is what I think captures the essence of a powerful set of values that resonate as high performance. This is from the firm's statements on sustainability:

"One of the most central traits of Nordic architecture is an insistence on high quality: towns and buildings must be attractive in a durable way . . . . Nordic architecture is anything but extravagant. Simplicity and sound finances are key, as is the ability to create architecture within a limited budget by using the relatively few resources available in an artistic way."

Henning Lassen has no formal value statement but seems to value an interdisciplinary and efficient approach to social and economic sustainability. They also support the U.N.'s Global Compact and Denmark's independent Green Think Tank CONCITO, and they led the organization of a summer school for architecture students in Damascus. Again, even though they don't articulate these as values, they are, and they seem to resonate from the staff.

Schmidt Hammer Lassen has a value statement on its Web page about architecture but expresses firm cultural values in terms of its Scandinavian heritage: "The practice is deeply rooted in the Scandinavian architectural traditions based on democracy, welfare, aesthetics, light, sustainability and social responsibility." They too support the U.N.'s Global Compact.

Honesty and Humanity

Although I enjoyed seemingly frank dialogue with each of these firms, and the Danes have an international reputation for both their honesty and human concerns, I don't have the knowledge to comment on how that actually plays out in these practices.

Curiosity

All of these firms seemed inherently curious in my encounters with them, though only a couple articulated a specific approach or development program for it.

3XN has created its research function specifically to enrich its projects with the latest technological, material, and sustainable possibilities. One obvious example where this came into play is the green sculpture in the garden of the Louisiana Museum, made of interactive and biological materials for which the firm won a JEC Innovation Award.

Arkitema demonstrates its approach to encouraging curiosity in many aspects of its practice. It maintains an education and knowledge portal called Arkidemy. Shortly after a merger with another firm (AA Arkitekter) Arkitema's leaders took the entire firm to a remote location to explore the new cultural reality and set precepts for a new physical location. The firm won a contract to explore new concepts for collaboration in construction (1995). It recently sent its youngest partners to a remote location to rethink the firm's future, and the list goes on.

BIG seems inherently curious in its approach to find new problems to solve rather than waiting for clients to define them.

Henning Larsen specifically addresses Curiosity as part of its approach: "Curiosity, high ambition and open working methods constitute the fundamentals of our best and most innovative designs."

Risk and Safe Failure

Because these firms get most or at least a substantial part of their work from (invited or pre-qualified) design competitions, there is an inherent acceptance of risk in the practice. Beyond that, it is not apparent to what degree personal risk taking (to develop new ideas or directions) is supported. Here, I suspect the collaborative ethos and the notions of Jante Law (defined earlier as "Don't think you are better than anyone else") may be an inhibitor to that type of self-initiative.

Shared Responsibility

Generally, these firms do not seem to embrace a concept of shared responsibility. I was a bit surprised by this because I thought the Danish ethos might push them that way, and I thought I saw a little of that when I worked with Norwegian firms. This was one of the biggest departures I saw in these firms from the aspects of habitat that I think are critical.

3XN's description of how they work suggests that they do not have a culture of shared responsibility: "managerial functions are the responsibility of the experienced senior architects in the team ... project teams are composed of staff with a variety of expert competencies to ensure that every assignment is carried out optimally."

C.F.Moller may be the exception in embracing shared responsibility, and they state their philosophy succinctly: "It is not a question of individual, personal achievement, but rather a process where everyone strives for a common architectural goal."

Collaboration

All six firms seemed to have a collaborative nature that was more implicit than articulated.

Nielsen of **3XN** responded that of course collaborative team participation was present, but that teams were "strongly led by partners."

Arkitema emphasizes their collaboration with users through the process they call "Arkitema Sensemaking."

BIG does not articulate collaboration but seems to practice it, internally for sure, and externally in their approach to seek out and solve for opposing points of view.

C.F. Moller is quite articulate about it, saying the firm "created buildings primarily through close cooperation within the practice as well as with clients and fellow design consultants. It is not a question of individual, personal achievement."

Henning Lassen states: "Our competencies are continuously being developed ... in the cross-disciplinary teamwork with collaborators and specialists from all over the world."

Schmidt Hammer Lassen describes their way of working as being "alongside our collaborators."

Without consciously working at it, these firms, to varying degrees, had much of the foundation in values for high design performance habitat. Risk and safe failure and shared responsibility were the weakest aspects in my view. Each of them is in a strong position to push for consistent high-performance design.

PURPOSE

A common sense of worthy purpose is an essential unifier for any high-performance culture. Most architects' individual perspective on the purpose of design is shaped by the pedagogy they encounter in school and after that by the nature of their practice experience. Their purpose is typically based on their values and their reaction to those experiences. In starting a practice, they may not give a lot of thought to it, operating under an implicit understanding. It is often only after a practice has established itself that the need to be clear about purpose seems important.

The purpose of high-performance design emerges from dealing with projects that have multiple stakeholders, that will touch a lot of users (private, public, or both), and in which clients desire to transform or increase their enterprise performance.

A declaration of purpose should encompass the things that are important to the impact the practice wants to have on the world and yet be realistic in terms of what it actually does. Following are some of the things that come to my mind as important considerations in purpose.

Experience better than that displaced. Since every realized building project shapes the environment, a serious part of design responsibility is to do no harm — that is, to ensure that each project is at least as positive for the ecosystem participant's experience as that which it displaced. While I mean that seriously, it would be disingenuous if we didn't admit that, in spite of an understanding of the planet's biodiversity, we still have a human-centric viewpoint no matter how sincere we are.

Authorship of caring and craft. At the core of why many of us chose to become designers is the desire to create spatial, visual, haptic experiences that are inspiring to human perception. This is where all of our skills in form-making, materiality, economy, craft, empathy, and art come into play. Our authorship is in the uniqueness of the solution as it resolves all of the influences at play in a way that comes from caring consideration of possibilities and execution of appropriate choice.

Authorship for some architects can be intertwined with personal perspective, which imprints solutions on multiple projects. This can add value or not, depending on its influence on the experience.

The brand of many leading designers is inherent in their expression of form and craft of execution, easily recognized in the work of Frank Gehry's firm or Richard Meier's. If the work is strongly based on client transformation, it is less likely to create such a strong form-based brand. Jerry Hirshberg described NDI as establishing a signature style of "an 'exo-structure' that, combined with taut but subtly nuanced three-dimensional forms ... achieved a signature style." But he went on to say that as that style approach was applied to the firm's second generation of designs for Nissan, in what they thought was "another level of maturity and refinement, it was received with disappointment. It did not bring the hoped for surprise and transformation ... the 'NDI look' had become the 'NDI smell' ... ."[24] A form-focused brand has its downside in pursuing high-performance design.

Authorship is also accomplished by collaboration of multiple personalities, skills, and stakeholders. If well led and enabled, this can produce powerful results. An authorship signature in this case can come from leadership personality, process, or a consistent approach to materiality and craft. So the question for every practice is, *How do you wish to have authorship and signature enter into your sense of purpose?*

Transformation and optimization. A designer's responsibility is to make the best and most sustainable use of all the resources committed to the work of creating built environment. There is almost universal agreement that our species has had the greatest impact on the planet and that we are exhausting many resources that are not renewable. To prolong our successful existence, we must be much more efficient and effective in our use of resources. That is the core of green building and sustainability. Beyond what those concepts normally include, however, we need to be effective in the use of human and economic resources as well as material resources. Economics is the engine for enabling all of our intervention. Human resources, which are threatened by age imbalance, unhealthy lifestyles, and abject poverty, are the means of implementation. Buildings shape the effectiveness and healthiness of the activities they house for as long as they exist. To be responsible, they must be both optimized for initial uses and adaptable for future change.

Ensuring this requires a transformative approach to design.

Building projects are infrequent events for most enterprises, and events that should require enterprises to analyze their entire being to match the building to

24 Hirshberg, *op. cit.*, p. 114-115.

the needs of their future. This makes the design process an ideal opportunity for enterprise transformation — optimizing organizationally and culturally to its vision for the future — which can be a rewarding aspect of design purpose.

Broad sustainability. A building is one of an enterprise's most expensive tools, with people and information systems the other top competitors for resources. At another level, basic shelter can be one of the most important survival tools for humankind. Buildings are essential, but they consume vast amounts of resources. So how can they be sustainable?

A broad sustainable purpose might have three aspects to it:

- Make sure that the resources that these endeavors commit contribute to the long-term effectiveness of the enterprise or the betterment of the human condition (justify the use).
- Ensure minimization and renewability of the resources used (the green aspect of sustainability).
- Eliminate the waste in the process of creating (design and construction).

It is not moral or rational to do otherwise.

Purpose can be directed broadly as an attitude and intent toward any issue, such as Arup's "We shape a better world." Or it can be focused on a narrower range of issues with great clarity. A focused purpose might be architecture in response to human crisis as chronicled in *Design Like You Give a Damn*[25] or it could focus on cultural, creative, or scientific endeavors. Purpose is likely to evolve over time as conditions in the world and capabilities of the design enterprise change. It is important to recognize change and embrace it. How you define purpose within this spectrum of worthy endeavors is less important to ultimate success than the sincerity and passion you have for whatever your definition is and the clarity with which you articulate and pursue it.

It is not a time to be timid about what design is capable of accomplishing. Daniel Pink, in his book *A Whole New Mind*, argues convincingly that we have evolved through agrarian to industrial to information ages and are now moving to the conceptual age in which the skills of design will add the most value and dealing with complexity will require Renaissance teams more than isolated genius.

[25] *Architecture for Humanity*, ed., New York, Metropolis Books, 2006.

Architect and former U.S. congressman and ambassador to Denmark Richard Swett, in his book *Leadership by Design*, demonstrated the validity and value of a design approach to solving issues of broad organizational and political importance.

Whatever the enterprise purpose is, to enable high performance, it must be worthy enough to generate passion in design. Your understanding of purpose will determine what you are designing your practice to do.

Purpose at NBBJ

NBBJ was founded in 1943 by a merger of three specialty practices. Floyd Naramore and 'Doc' Brady's practice focused on education, William Bain's practice focused on housing, and Perry Johanson's practice focused on health care. Thus, from its beginning, this architectural design practice had a multi-specialty focus on what many designers would consider program-driven design.

When I joined the firm in 1965, the range of specialties had grown (adding corporate / commercial and laboratory research), but the underlying multi-specialty approach to program-intensive buildings was still intact. The purpose (and vision) of the firm at that time (1967) read: "... Promote effective and efficient use of management and manpower resources in order for the firm to maintain its competitive position with other firms."

Get inspired by that if you can! Or find yourself as a client!

In my early years as a designer and in my first few years as a partner in the firm, that basic sense (lack?) of purpose was not challenged, and the focus was on improving the aesthetic quality of the work, eliminating barriers to successful implementation, and examining and sometimes emulating the practice habits of firms we admired (e.g., SOM and Caudill Rowlett & Scott). We were improving the way we approached a rather loosely defined purpose.

We did, however, begin to understand that we were trying to change the environment of the practice. The purpose and vision became in 1975: "... Create a professional environment which will support and nourish creativity, recognize human worth and dignity, and provide as a consequence, excellence in architecture and its related disciplines at a reasonable profit." Well, a little more about creativity but still a highly self-focused idea of purpose.

It wasn't until we felt significant success in establishing higher design performance that we began to understand the need to rethink the basic purpose of the firm. That was in the mid 1980s. At first we didn't even have an articulate language to use in thinking about purpose, and we struggled with notions of beauty, client, and staff satisfaction and the like. We expressed our mission at that time (1987) as:

- "Beautiful Buildings and Environment,

- Satisfied Customers,
- Personal, Professional and Financial Satisfaction,
- Contribute to a Better Society."

Our clients had finally entered the picture along with a bit of social purpose.

Our vision at the time was: "Dedicated to excellence in analysis and design of our built environment."

A little more aspirational but still not very focused. It was, however, beginning to awaken dialogue in the firm. And the recent changes in the firm to an open environment, flattening of the hierarchy, and emphasis on design performance were enabling and enriching that dialogue.

In our next evolution, we placed high emphasis on our aspirations for what we were questing to become. By 1991, this vision was expressed: "Be the best large design firm in the world."

The internal effect of this was immediate and powerful. Initial reactions ranged from groans to rigorous debate about what "best" meant and why "large." The rigorous debate carried the groaners into it and provided a design focus to prospect-, project-, and practice-related dialogues for a long time.

By 1996 we expanded the vision: "Be the best design firm in the world."

We had initially thought "large" helped to define the complex nature of our projects, but later felt it was a cop out.

During this focus on becoming, the purpose or mission statement was at first loosely defined. Even though this vision was not purpose-focused, it was a strong instrument of transformation for us, largely because of the loud, participatory, and rigorous dialogue it fostered. This was enhanced because we made a rigorous and continuous effort to evaluate our actions and designs against the criteria of making progress toward this vision. It became a serious discussion of the purpose of design and contributed to redefining ourselves.

Initially, the purpose (mission statement) that related to these visions of being the best was: "To provide the highest value to clients, society, and the firm."

As we continued to examine what value really was and recognized the responsibility assumed in committing the resources that a building requires, we began to think more seriously about the consequences of outcome. Initially, one of our partners, Rick Buckley, who became managing partner for design before his untimely death, pushed on the issue of content (both rational and emotional) to create a basis for meaningful form. This was a pretty useful concept in critiquing our work because it provided a concrete commodity to look for: relevance ... including, but more than aesthetics ... that made a difference that mattered to users, owners, and society.

About that time I received one of those valuable "Aha" messages from a client, Blair Sadler, an attorney by training and at that time CEO of Children's Hospital and Health Center in San Diego. We were in Stockholm and had both given presentations that day, mine on a new health care building typology we were working on and Blair's on his hospital's project (which we had designed) and his work with the Center for Health Design. As we were walking through Gamla Stan that June evening on our way back to the hotel, Blair said to me (in the nicest possible way): "Jim, you really ought to speak more from your clients' and their customers' and neighbors' perspective when you talk about architecture. You do great work, but if I want to understand why it should mean anything to me, I want to know what it does more than what it is." Nice wakeup call, Blair. Thank you.

And as we continuously looked at our work and assessed what we thought was the "best," we realized that the most valuable of our work was creating significant positive change for its users, owners, neighbors, and occasionally, we opined, for society by creating new models.

Initiated by a creative analysis done by planning and economics partner Bill Sanford, with the planning focused studio, we adopted a brand statement that was purpose-laden and covered the intent of our work nicely:

"We are Artists of Change

- Fearlessly Creative
- Collaboratively Developed
- Intelligently Realized"

This led to a minor adjustment in purpose thinking to: "... Creating extraordinary value for clients, the firm and society."

And a couple of years later, as we began to think on a more global environmental scale, it became: " … Creating extraordinary value for clients, the firm, society and life."

During this time and based on our recognition of the transformative aspect of the best work, we began to develop a monograph on the transformative nature of architecture, an effort led by partners Scott Wyatt, Tim Johnson, Rich Dallam, and head of PR Helen Dimoff working with Bruce Mau's firm. That effort involved mining the creative thinking of all 67 of the firm's principals, starting with the question, "When it's as good as it gets, what are we doing?" The process was purposely provocative, including a working title/theme "Fire the Architects," and led to the participatory crafting of the firm's vision and a book[26], one truly written from the clients' perspective and in a large part from their own words. This book has become the clearest definition of purpose ever for the firm and the easiest to disseminate throughout. Not so incidentally, it has been a great marketing tool and has recently been updated and republished. The book's title is double entendre for dual purpose: our clients' need to change their enterprises and the profession's need to embrace design as a tool for client success.

Having a clear sense of purpose that can be used to assess design on a day-to-day basis has been important for NBBJ, and the dialogue within the firm over worthy purpose was in itself a focusing tool for pursuit of high performance.

[26] *Change Design: Conversations about Architecture as the Ultimate Business Tool*, Atlanta, Greenway Communications, 2006.

Purpose in Danish Firms

One sense of purpose that permeates all of these firms is a democratic notion of architecture's role in serving people. I am sure that comes from the national value system and is in the unconscious background for some. Others articulate it very well.

Kim Herforth Nielsen of **3XN** describes the firm's purpose as "creating behavior" through design. That theme is expanded in the firm's recent exhibit at the Danish Design Center, where seven "behaviors" are explored: social, cultural, building, public, responsible, learning, and human. There is a further purpose articulated for the firm's research arm, **GXN**, which is to apply the latest knowledge and technology to 3XN architecture.

Arkitema defines its vision in a way that I would call "purpose instead":

- Building Sustainable...both sustainable and competitive
- Building Customized...getting behind the stated needs through anthropological investigation and aesthetics
- Building Smart...pushing the edges of technology in construction.

And "Our goal is to create value for our customers, for the users, and for society as a whole."

BIG's purpose, though I did not find it explicitly articulated as such, is to translate society's issues into a physical form. That is expressed in Yes Is More as "BIG operates in the fertile margin between the two opposites ... (naively utopian or petrifyingly pragmatic) ... A pragmatic utopian architecture that takes on the creation of socially, economically, and environmentally perfect places as a practical objective."[27] Ingels has a way with words, and his attitude seems to permeate BIG's staff.

For **C.F. Moller**, purpose seems centered on "an animated and evolving architecture that applauds simplicity, clarity, and unpretentiousness, but also diversity" (drawn from their vision statement). They also describe a goal of "being recognized globally and to be among the best practices in Scandinavia and Europe ... setting new standards for design and construction of buildings ... developing new models for procurement and collaboration."

[27] Bjarke Ingels Group, i, p. 12.

Purpose for **Henning Larsen** can be traced to its founder and summed up by "Change the world." Beyond that they have a "goal to create engaging, sustainable projects that reach beyond themselves and become of durable value to user, the society, and the culture they are built into."

Schmidt Hammer Lassens' purpose is also expressed as a vision statement: "Our vision is to optimize the value of the user's space. We develop integrated end to end solutions of the highest quality in constant search for new ways and answers." But perhaps more meaningful now are summaries from its "green manifesto 2007" and "architecture manifesto 2008": "schmidt hammer lassen architecture is all about creating a better setting for people's lives and development, and it is also about seeing nature and the world's resources from a globally sustainable perspective. As architects we have both the opportunity and the responsibility to design a better world .... schmidt hammer lassen architecture intends to create space and titillate the senses using elements of surprise and poetry. We push the boundaries with our unstinting curiosity, and we always seek the solution that is ultimately the best in qualitative as well as artistic, conceptual, technical, and economic terms."

The real impact of a firm's purpose is uniting its people around their passion. Therefore, the most effective purpose is that which is passionately demonstrated by firm leaders and relevant to staff. All six of these firms show passion for their work, and that passion is aligned well with staff in part at least because the majority embrace the Danish ethos. The biggest, hairiest expression is Henning Larsen's "Change the world," and that seems to carry passion with the firm's leaders. BIG's push to build on the opportunities of potential conflict, while harder to encapsulate, seems deeply ingrained in that firm's relatively young staff.

PARTICIPATION

Participation is an essential motivator for creative people. If they do not feel engaged in the design process in a way that allows them to shape the nature of the questions pursued and influence the outcome, they will soon disengage themselves from the projects or the enterprise. Sir Ove Arup stated it in "The Key Speech," "If he finds after a while that he is frustrated by red tape or by having someone breathing down his neck, someone for whom he has little respect, if he has little influence on decisions which affect his work and which he may not agree with, then he will pack up and go. And he should."[28]

Participation in a design practice is important at many levels, but early in a design career it is most important at the project level. As a designer gains experience and begins to understand all of the issues that affect the achievement of a high-performance design he or she will become more concerned about participation in shaping a much broader part of the design practice.

The way a project team is organized and the way it behaves determine whether the team achieves a real sense of participation. Each team member must feel that his or her ideas are heard and that he or she has an influence in the choice of ideas that get pursued and a role in the development of those ideas. Having this, each team member will feel a shared sense of ownership of the design and will be motivated to make it the best it can be. This cannot, however, become a collective or even a democratic approach. It demands clear and strong leadership to draw out, select, and sell the best ideas. Creative people will be even more disengaged if they see that the process is without strong and convincing leadership and that ideas get watered down rather than built upon and strengthened by the process. Making this work depends upon confident, empathetic, and well listening leadership as well as a culture of excellence-seeking and curiosity.

This is worth repeating: The way a firm is organized and the way it behaves determine a person's sense of participation in practice direction. Key concerns for designers are the nature of the design projects pursued and won; the nature of the relationships with clients (contractual and otherwise) which influence the likelihood of success or failure; and the financial model the firm pursues and how that model supports the projects (most important) and how it supports development and fair compensation. Open presentation of the

[28] Sir Ove Arup, *op. cit.*

facts and open discussion (dialogue not monologue) of the firm's values and strategy are key tools in providing the sense of participation. This will bring us to the next point: communication.

Participation at NBBJ

In the economic downturn of the early 1980s, NBBJ went through a rough patch in financial performance, which awakened us (rudely) to realize that we were not practicing with adequate financial responsibility and rigor. This was about the time that I became CEO for the western two-thirds of our practice. We needed to take rapid and far-reaching steps to get on a more sound footing. To do this, our CFO and I went into a deep charrette of analysis and system design focused on achieving fiscal rigor but from a project-success perspective (what systems would be helpful to the projects and, importantly but clearly secondary, provide firm leadership with tools to improve rigor). To accomplish these changes we held dialogues with firm and project leadership and with the entire staff. We explained what the issues were and what our analysis suggested would make it better, and we shared our concern that it would take all of us to fix it. We needed their critique of what we were suggesting as well as their ideas. We got ideas and critique (as well as a lot of blame and some flame mail) that gave us a basis for modifying and refining an approach. Additional rounds of dialogue were held, and within a few months we had an overwhelming buy-in to a very rigorous change in systems and behavior. That led to an ongoing goal-based approach to improve financial rigor and performance, which was nonetheless always viewed as support to the pursuit of design excellence. This could not have happened if the whole firm had not participated meaningfully in the process.

We have made extensive use of 360-degree performance evaluation techniques at all levels of the firm (including managing partners) to make the performance review and coaching process participatory. To make it objective and anonymous, we used outside compilers (James P. Cramer's Greenway Group). We have always emphasized the coaching and self-discovery aspects of this process to enhance performance rather than just critique it. Outside objectivity is particularly sensitive at the partner level as we learned one year when it was felt that one partner might have had inappropriate access to the reviews, which caused a lot of discomfort with the process, damaging its effectiveness that year considerably.

We have pushed participation in the promotion process into the firm's structure by starting it each year with a process of peer nominations. The process filters up to the principals for decisions, but studios are the most influential in the process. The annual state-of-the-firm dialogues are a visible way to garner participation from all staff in the firm — during the dialogues themselves, from the more outspoken, which provided an agenda for more private individual dialogues.

Participation in Danish Firms

All six firms seem to have a participatory approach to design, but three seem to have made the practice more specific and more inclusive of all aspects of their practices. **Arkitema** has consciously involved its whole staff in an exploration of firm culture and its youngest leaders in defining future directions. **BIG**, with the intimacy of the office environment and the playful attitude of the leadership, seems to engage everyone in everything the firm is about.

And **Schmidt Hammer Lassen**, in its exploration of the transition to a new generation, spent more than a year with a large group of potential firm leaders examining the future of architecture and the purpose of the firm, producing three manifestos describing its views of the future and the firm's approach to it.

There is a socially mandated program of continuing education for everyone, funded by the firms, which provides a source of opportunity to learn together. Several of these firms use this as one means of having learning experiences together that build a sense of community and mutual understanding.

COMMUNICATION

Communication is the lifeblood of any organization and critical in a high-performance environment. Communication takes many forms, and unfortunately, it will always be true that whatever level of communication exists, it will not satisfy everyone. Many will feel left out in some way important to them, and a few may feel that their time is wasted in over-communication. As Jerry Hirshberg puts it: "There are what seem to be two mutually contradictory and often-heard cries from within an organization. On the one hand, there is a reasonable plea for clear understanding of the responsibilities and limits of a job, position, or department. On the other hand, there is an urgent need to feel connected with the overall picture and the end product."[29]

Finding the best means and level of communication is a major concern for a designing enterprise. It requires conscious design and a lot of trial and error, and it is not a constant in any organization. Different market, social, and economic climates demand different approaches. Personal communication at a one-on-one level carries the most weight with individuals, and every level in a progression from individual to group to mass communication has value for the right kind of communication. But, at some level, it transitions from meaningful dialogue to unidirectional messaging. Messaging is needed at times and is critical to timely information sharing. In a participatory culture, dialogue is the means best suited for achieving full mutual understanding and buy-in. Cost of communication tends to be inversely proportional to how broadband it is.

Content of communication must match the values, purpose, and culture of an enterprise. If design excellence is the *raison d'être*, then communication should be dominated by that (though there may be times when critical financial, ethical, or market issues must take the focus for brief periods).

---

29 Hirshberg, *op. cit.*, p.138.

Communication at NBBJ

When I joined NBBJ, communication was pretty much what it was at other firms into which I had insight through friends (i.e., it was sporadic, not particularly focused, most often reactive, and generally only dealt with issues to be celebrated, not necessarily the most important issues of concern to staff).

After I became a partner and as we struggled with our early efforts to design ourselves, we tried many ways of communicating our values and intentions. We did not have any clear ideas about open information sharing and dealt with most issues as messaging softened by celebrations to follow.

On one occasion when we had been expensively pursuing Middle East markets for a long time with no success, we got a verbal commitment from a client (a distant relative of the royal family) on a project that sounded sweet. In an effort to assure doubtful staff that this market effort was indeed worthy, the partner in charge and the CFO put on an in-office celebration announcing this great success. They dressed in keffiyeh, akal, and flowing jellabas and, with cymbals banging, served up a passable Middle Eastern feast. It was fun. But as the months went by and the possibility of the project faded, it seemed ludicrous, and we lost valuable staff trust in our judgment and honesty. It was an embarrassing but important lesson.

Over time we developed a menu of many types of communication. Some were regular, with predictable content, others were irregular but with predictable focus, and others were situation tailored. Some were done for full firm audiences but most were for smaller, more dialogue-enabled groups. These included:

- Annual state-of-the-firm presentations and dialogue (managing partners in person at each location)
- Annual promotion/awards celebrations, (Web connected firm-wide)
- Periodic "town hall" meetings at studio and office levels
- Firm-wide principals meetings/issue charrettes
- Small-group breakfasts between managing partners and recent hires
- Office wide presentation/discussions with stimulating outsiders
- Many issue- and discipline-focused group discussions, workshops, and retreats.

The small-group breakfast discussions are valuable in a number of ways. We would do these after a person had been with us for at least three months but no more than nine. We told them that this was because we wanted to hear their views after they had been able to form an opinion but before they had been over-indoctrinated. The size of the group was typically five or six new hires and one or two managing partners. Since we would always take the time to give a five-minute bio-sketch of ourselves (new hires and managing partners alike) it gave us a chance to explore in some depth the nature of the people we were bringing into the firm. We learned about their unique interests, both related and unrelated to design, and the prior design experiences they brought, from which we could learn. We learned why they had come to NBBJ and differences, both positive and negative, between NBBJ and their prior experience. We also used it as a chance to share our purpose and values, and what our expectations were of them, as well as what we thought they could expect of us. These were as open a dialogue exchange as we could make them. And because they usually included seasoned new hires as well as younger ones, the perspectives were quite varied.

The town hall-type meetings were initiated by Scott Wyatt when he stepped into a managing partner role, and he made them effective in getting at issues on people's minds and drawing out ideas to take us forward.

Communication in Danish Firms

These firms seem to have a reasonably communicative internal atmosphere and spatial environments that enable open involvement, and all of them have elegant Web sites that communicate a sense of purpose well.

3XN effectively uses videos of founding partner Kim Herforth Nielsen discussing their work. They describe their work as a network structure, continuously interchanging ideas and staff between their two offices. Their internal communication includes videoconferences between Aarhus and Copenhagen offices; ongoing workshops; an annual theme day for all staff, where both offices gather for a day of inspiration, teambuilding, etc.; daily updates on the firm's intranet, INPUT Thursdays every three weeks with external speakers such as Consul from Dubai, a philosopher, or new innovative manufacturers; and a monthly office meeting with general updates on projects, competitions, social events, etc.

BIG's archicomic "Yes Is more"[30] provides a very effective internal communication of values and purpose, and Ingels' personal interactive style and articulateness engage the staff well.

C.F. Moller Managing Partner Tom Danielsen says that they are extremely communicative among their offices, keeping staff informed and sharing ideas.

None of the other firms described a conscious strategy for communication, other than **Schmidt Hammer Lassen's** approach to creating manifestos, described above. Nevertheless, each of these firms seemed to communicate well internally, and staff I talked with seemed to feel connected.

---

[30] Bjarke Ingels Group, *op. cit.*

APPROACH

By approach, I mean the basic actions the design firm believes are essential to achieving design success. These are generally broad categories of activities, not the tailored actions that make up a process plan for a specific project. An approach is the structured attitude that you bring to the design event as well as to the practice. The importance of this is to ensure effectiveness: that the basic ingredients to powerful design are always included in project efforts and that something critical is not overlooked or ignored. And it is important to ensure efficiency: that priorities are established in what to explore and decision making is timely. Approach provides the guardrails for consistency in a high-performance environment.

Amabile[31] cites Helmholtz and Wallas describing models of the creative process (what I would call approaches) consisting of:

Helmholtz:

- Saturation (gathering facts)
- Incubation (considering new combinations)
- Illumination (a glimpse of the solution)

And Wallas:

- Preparation
- Incubation
- Illumination
- Verification

Amabile goes on to create her "componential model of creativity," which consists of:

- Problem identification
- Preparation

---

[31] Amabile, *op. cit.*, p.99.

- Response generation
- Response validation and communication

Tom Kelley of the design firm IDEO describes the firm's methodology as having five steps:

1. Understand (market, client, technology, constraints)
2. Observe (real people, situations)
3. Visualize (new to world concepts, customers)
4. Evaluate and refine (prototype iteration)
5. Implement (commercialization)[32]

A high pH firm, whether designing products or buildings, must have an approach that includes, as a minimum, an attitude about investigation and definition, ideation and analysis, and implementation and realization.

32 Kelley, Tom, *op. cit.*, p. 6-7.

Approach at NBBJ

The approach at NBBJ evolved to the idea of an overlapping continuum of discover, design, and deliver, focused on experience, form, and craft. This is in pursuit of high performance, which we call change design. The diagram in Figure 2 represents this approach.

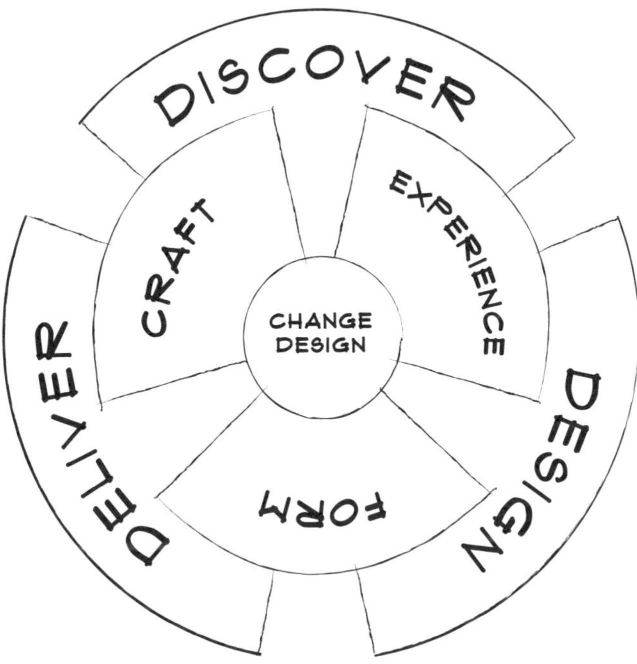

Figure 2. *NBBJ approach: discover, design, deliver*

Discovery entails investigation of client purpose and dreams, site and social context and influence, precedents and transformational opportunities, metrics of success along with existing baseline metrics, development of the story of project purpose, and definition of successful outcome including enterprise impact, cost, and time. Co-discovery with clients is part of this and is where the purpose of the project can be molded into high-performance design potential.

Design involves developing precepts (guiding principles) that can be molded into the project story, development, modeling, testing, and sorting of concepts (physical and non-physical), and evolutionary development and refinement to a solution. In most recent times, the design process includes development of construction and fabrication strategy as well. Here too, co-design with clients is important, both in finding the transformative solution and in using the process to help transform the clients' culture.

Delivery includes the process of client transformation through the design process as well as building actualization through fabrication and construction. Collaboration of owner, designer, and builder is essential to us, and we push for all three. On almost all of the work we rate as high-performance design, we have had that three-way collaboration.

Approach in Danish Firms

3XN describes its approach in the title of the monograph "Investigate, Ask, Tell, Draw, Build."[33] Its approach to architecture is based on a process of investigating the culture, place, and context of the site; asking the relevant questions of those whom the building is about; and then creating the story to tell about the building and why it is relevant before drawing; and finally building the structure.

Arkitema calls its approach "Sensemaking: integrated building and organizational design," which it describes as aesthetic and anthropological, including five aspects:

1. Defining
2. Discovering
3. Dreaming
4. Designing
5. Delivering

It describes its approach as one of co-design with users/clients.

BIG describes an approach of excess (of ideas and criteria) and a Darwinian survival process of selection and mutation, a process that is highly participatory and inclusive.

Bjarke Ingels views this as a responsible approach to architectural evolution, embracing all conflicting demands in a process that evolves through the gymnastics of finding compatibility (not compromise) between seemingly polarized demands.

C.F. Moller does not articulate an approach with any specificity but rather relies on dialogue and shared philosophy.

Henning Larsen is also rather non-specific in describing its approach as based on four concepts: idea development, quality of collaboration, project management, and quality assurance.

Schmidt Hammer Lassen views its approach as workshop-based, encompassing multiple viewpoints, gaining total team understanding and buy-in. It brings its core values to the project but focuses on getting to the core essence of the specific

33 3XN Architects, London, Black Dog Publishing, 2007.

project. This is done by a pre-analysis performed by senior design staff who seek to discover the DNA of the project and express it in a set of "value words," which become both mantra and totem for the project.

Approaches within these firms thus ranges from very specific to very loose, and generally is project specific, but none expresses a conscious method of designing project-specific approaches.

PROJECTS

Definition and Discovery, Ideation, Delivery and Implementation, Process, Tools

Projects are the most important issue for a high pH design enterprise. They are what the enterprise is created to do. If there is one thing that must be right in the design of a designing enterprise, it is that the enterprise ensures consistent high creativity in its projects and continuous improvement in their implementation.

Projects start with a definition of what the project is and what it is to accomplish. That definition has often been limited to a program, or brief, created by a client or client's consultant. These programs have rarely been adequate to achieve a high-performance design, which demands an exploration of enterprise purpose and potential for transformation as well as an understanding of the opportunities of the project context.

Projects involve investigation and discovery of relevant information ranging from facts of influence (codes, costs, climate, context, etc.) to explorations of user behaviors and desires, to precedents and new developments in relatable fields.

Projects involve a process of ideation, selection, mutation, and refinement. This is the core of the design process, yet few designing entities have spent time in ideation about how to optimize this activity. This may be one of the greatest areas of potential performance improvement for high design performance enterprises.

Projects are meaningless unless they are fully realized, meaning that they are implemented in a way that fulfills all of the intentions of the design and transformation. This requires a collaboration with builders and fabricators that is well beyond the bounds of traditional contract administration agreements.

DEFINITION AND DISCOVERY

The adage "Do the right thing and then do the thing right" is a key principle of high pH practice. Discovering the right thing is a process that too often gets cut short because of time pressure or fee structure, because of traditional attitudes about the responsibility of the client to provide the program or brief, because of a lack of real curiosity, and sometimes by the reliability-over-validity bias described in Roger Martin's book.[34] But a high-performance design cannot happen unless there is a deep understanding of the issues being addressed socially, organizationally, and technologically. As Jerry Hirshberg says: "Designers are notoriously quick at drawing their pencils and firing away at solutions. When confronted with a situation for which there is no immediately obvious answer, there is a great temptation for any professional to move too quickly into a problem-solving mode ... ."[35]

It is critical that the process of gathering and absorbing both the directly related influences and potentially applicable precedents happens before a leap into ideation. This does not mean that the discovery of relevant and useful ideas shouldn't be expressed as precepts, or pre-design ideas that can be used to inform design, but it does mean that there is great danger and potential for wasted time if not outright failure in falling for seductive form before understanding the broadest implications of performance needs.

Developing effective, inclusive, and expansive discovery techniques and having the creative skill to define the problem with clear and agreed objectives are essential to laying the foundation for a high-performance design. This necessarily must be a collaborative effort with client and user. And critically, these techniques must be efficient for the design team and especially so for the client team. A strong sense of agreed purpose established among user, designers, and makers is also important.

IDEATION

Ideation, the process of developing design solutions, is the creative core value that design can deliver. Brilliant ideation is the sine qua non of a high pH firm and high-performance designs. This is what a culture must enable, empower, and optimize.

How to define creativity, however, is subject to a lot of analysis and interpretation. A common definition used by neuro-researchers is "the ability to combine novelty and usefulness in a particular social context."[36]

---

[34] Martin, Roger, *The Design of Business*, Boston, Harvard Business Press, 2009, p. 42.

[35] Hirshberg, *op. cit.*, p. 81.

[36] Cohen, Patricia, "Charting Creativity: Signposts of a Hazy Territory," *New York Times*, May 8, 2010, p. C1.

Psychologist Rollo May provides a very broad definition: "Actual creativity I define as the process of bringing something new into birth."[37] He also says "Creativity ... is the encounter of the intensively conscious human being with his world."[38]

Another psychologist in the creative field, Carl Rogers, defines the creative process as "the emergence in action of a novel relational product, growing out of the uniqueness of the individual on the one hand, and the materials, events, people, or circumstances of life on the other."[39]

Design leader and artist Jerry Hirshberg is much more specific: "For me, creative thought is, and always has been, the marriage of passion and logic, intuition and information, free imagination and the discipline of mastered skills."[40] And, more poetically, he states: "Creativity is the mastery of information and skills in the service of dreams."[41]

More important to this discussion than defining creativity is understanding how to create a habitat that stimulates it. Work by Dr. Rex Jung at the Mind Research Network has suggested that creativity may follow a slower and less direct pathway through the brain than intelligence: "Although intelligence and skill are generally associated with the fast and efficient firing of neurons, subjects who tested high in creativity had thinner white matter and connecting axons that have the effect of slowing nerve traffic in the brain. This slowdown ... might allow for the linkage of more disparate ideas, more novelty and more creativity."[42] So maybe if we can make our brains slow down we won't become so attached to the first or most obvious ideas.

Ideation is an aspect of high-performance design where more is better because more ideas from a broader perspective are likely to provide the ingredients for a richer and more relevant design. As James L. Adams, the Stanford University leader in creativity, said: "The more creative concepts you have to choose from, the better. This is true at all stages of the problem-solving process, whether you are attempting to decide upon a broad direction or imple-

37 May, Rollo, "The Nature of Creativity," essay in *Creativity and its Cultivation,* ed. Anderson, Harold H., New York, Harper & Row 1959, p. 57.

38 May, *ibid.,* p. 68.

39 Rogers, Carl A., "Toward a Theory of Creativity," essay in *Creativity and Its Cultivation*, ed. Anderson, Harold H., New York Harper & Row, 1959, p.71.

40 Hirshberg, *op. cit.*, p. 194.

41 Hirshberg, *op. cit.*, p. 212.

42 Cohen, Patricia, "Charting Creativity: Signposts of a Hazy Territory," *The New York Times*, May 8, 2010, p. C7.

ment a detailed solution."[43] And Tom Kelley quotes Linus Pauling: "The best way to get a good idea is to get a lot of ideas."[44]

But how can this be done?

There is a substantial body of theory, science (both social and psychological), and experiential advice that can be mined for ideas.

The bibliography in this book lists many of them, and some are encapsulated below. In general, the literature is heavier on identifying obstacles to creativity than it is on stimulants. Understanding both has value, and the maximum benefit will come from common-sense use of the most specifically applicable principles. Some basic principles repeated in much of this literature and the effectiveness of which coincide with my experience are:

1. **Align people with their passions.**
   While it is not likely practical to do this absolutely, it is not that difficult to do it much of the time, and the impact has a carry-over effect from project to project.
2. **Lead collaboratively (not collectively).**
   And enable significant leadership from every chair. The way to draw on talent is to encourage and guide it and to risk allowing it to step in front of you.
3. **Make critique a positive part of the process.**
   This means that it should be frequent, open, civil, fun, focused, and preferably non-binding but with accountability to peers a strong expectation.
4. **Selectively use heuristics.**
   Develop at least a minimum menu of creativity aids that you use both to loosen up the process and focus the search on a regular basis.
5. **Collaboratively design the process.**
   For this, see the chapter on process.
6. **Start with a clear and mutually owned (and mutable through discovery) objective.**
   For this, see definition/discovery above.
7. **Acknowledge that ideation is messy.**
   But if it is outcome-focused, it should not be chaotic

43 Adams, *op. cit.*, p. 7.

44 Kelley, *op. cit.*, p. 55.

8. Select solutions that are valid and will deliver on the promise.
And develop them reliably (within the parameters promised).

A high pH firm must find its own principles for ensuring that it is drawing the most it can from its design approach. Continuously being alert to and willing to test ways of enriching the creative thought process is an essential characteristic of a high pH habitat.

The following is a review of some of the published work on creativity that has provided insight.

Grudin

According to Robert Grudin, professor of English at the University of Oregon, "The special province of creative thought is to perceive and communicate form ... the operative principle of a given phenomenon ... . Creative thinking is philomorphic (form loving)."[45]

We designers would leap at this in thinking physical form, but Grudin is broader in his meaning of form as order whether physical or not.

"The word 'inspiration' originally meant a breath of divinity or transfusion of soul received from the gods by some deserving individual," Grudin writes. "The word now denotes the experience of a sudden insight that cuts across categories or otherwise leaps over the normal steps of reasoning." And it is the original one that he believes holds more psychological truth because: "To be inspired is to surrender one's mind to a new force, heedless and powerful."[46] Most of us have experienced this in the design process, and our goal in designing creative habitat is to enhance the probability of it happening for all design team members.

Grudin's book explores the sources of creative energy and the paths and pitfalls that lie between creative energy and effective innovation.

He says, "While inspiration and discovery concern different areas of experience, they are similar at heart. Both carry the same rush of adrenaline, the same giddiness, the same temporary loss of identity. To achieve both inspiration and discovery individuals must reconcile within themselves a number of

45 Grudin, Robert, *op. cit.*, p. 176.

46 Grudin, Robert, *ibid.*, p. 10.

classic dichotomies: knowledge and innocence, reason and emotion, conquest and surrender, subject and object, idea and matter … ."[47]

He identifies human characteristics (habits really) that form an ethos for inspiration:

- Passion for the work; a blurring of the boundary between work and leisure
- Fidelity to the work; complete concentration and focus
- Love of the problematic; vigorous and uncompromising in both getting the question right and seeking its solution
- Love of beauty; a unity between experience and mind
- A sense of wholeness; seeing or seeking the holistic relationships among all elements or aspects
- Boldness; courage to risk the ridiculous and pursue a good idea in spite of strangeness
- Consequence; being persistent and discerning that each event has value to the whole whether it is a success or a failure
- Innocence and playfulness; starting with the innocence of a clean slate and devoid of embarrassment
- Courtesy; appreciation, deference, humility toward ideas and detail
- Suffering; enduring contradiction, anomaly, criticism (and being strengthened, enlightened by it)
- Remembrance; respect for precedent, ability to draw analogy from the past
- A sense of the continuity of perception; making connections between ideas not previously seen that way
- A sense of openness; a trust that there is much that is unknown and much room for new ideas
- Liberty; seeing life and nature as necessarily mutable.

He describes discovery as normally occurring via "two main channels of cognition; analogy and anomaly." Analogy is the discovery of an unexpected underlying order or similarity; anomaly is the discovery of an unexpected disorder (something extra, something missing, or things out of order).

[47] Grudin, Robert, *ibid.*, p. 33.

He describes factors that hinder discovery as:

- Attempting to please or gain acceptance
- Expressing rebellion or anger
- Fear of change in our perception of reality, or repressed fear
- Great concern for self-fulfillment or self-expression
- Strong expectations of their reality
- Non-acceptance of the five senses
- Poor memory
- Low aspiration or non-belief in miracles
- Lack of humor
- Intellectual self-indulgence
- Over-focus on special strengths
- Competition with those around us

Some of this will seem familiar to many, but some of it will seem irrelevant to many, as well. For the latter, there is great value in exploring the things that don't seem relevant, for in them is the opportunity to discover a new way to heighten performance.

Hirshberg

Jerry Hirshberg's book *The Creative Priority: Driving Innovative Business in the Real World*[48] recounts the development of a high design performance habitat under his guidance as he founded and developed Nissan Design International (NDI). He says, "Unprecedented thinking often involves the holding of apparently disconnected, conflicting, overlapping, or even mutually exclusive thoughts in the mind simultaneously. By substituting the words 'people' or 'groups' for 'thoughts' in the previous sentence, it is possible to see creativity's potential as an organizing force for relationships as well as for information. In this way the shadow cast by two strongly divergent orientations is rendered irrelevant in the blinding light of their possible fusion into an utterly original perspective."[49]

---

[48] Hirshberg, op. cit.

[49] Hirshberg, *ibid.*, p. 22

His describes four themes for enhancing creative performance, which have permeated a set of 11 strategies or priorities that were developed at Nissan Design International under his leadership.

1. Polarity

- Creative abrasion; the incorporation rather than compromise of differences in viewpoint
- Divergent pairs; specifically hiring and pairing people for their differences in perspective
- Embracing the dragon; getting beyond the preconceived antipathies in an assignment and getting to the root creative possibilities by embracing the dual nature of reality

2. Boundary

- Blurring of disciplinary boundaries; spreading responsibility, contributing to design outside normally defined roles, and self-selection for contribution enhance creativity
- Intercultural creativity: treating diverse disciplines as alien cultures; embracing personality differences, being hard on issues, soft on people...
- Drinking from diverse wells; seeking problem variations at different scales (e.g., a car and a yacht), narrowing for expertise and refinement versus distancing for breadth and perspective

3. Unprecedented Thinking

- Creative questions before creative answers; asking the basic dumb questions to get a clear (and fresh) perspective
- Stepping back from the canvas; releasing tension by disrupting and distancing from the process
- Failure, cheating, and play; see possibilities in failures, pick up and build on others ideas, play around with them

4. Synthesis

- Informed intuition; getting beneath the statistics and shaping the future

- Porous planning; allowing the nonlinear, unanticipated breakthroughs
- Hirshberg set out to design a high design performance entity at NDI and succeeded grandly in a short period of time. He offers much to learn from.

Roger Martin

Roger Martin, dean of the Rotman School of Management at the University of Toronto, has focused on the need for "design thinking" as he calls it, in all kinds of enterprise ventures. He has authored two books on this subject, *The Opposable Mind*[50] and *The Design of Business*.[51] In the latter, he describes design thinking as the balance of analytical mastery and intuitive originality in dynamic interplay. He poses a polarity between demand for reliability, based on the past as evidence and validity based on future outcome. In describing the typical enterprise bias for reliability, he helps us understand the dilemma of acceptance of originality and provides useful ideas for dealing with it.

James L. Adams

Adams groundwork-laying book *Conceptual Blockbusting: A Guide to Better Ideas*[52] was one of the earliest books that I found to have applicable ideas about enabling and enhancing creativity.

He outlines several classes of impediments to creative thought, which he calls "conceptual blocks." The classes include:

- Perceptual blocks (such as stereotyping)
- Emotional blocks (such as fear of failure)
- Cultural and environmental blocks (such as taboos, distractions)
- Intellectual and expressive blocks (such as ineffective approach, inadequate information)

Adams reviews "alternate thinking languages" (verbal, mathematical, visual, and other sensory) that can enhance a creative process, and he discusses a range of "blockbusting" approaches. Some of his proposed creative thinking aids include "morphological forced connections" a "bug list" and a checklist

50 Martin, Roger, *The Opposable Mind*, Boston, Harvard Business Press, 2007.

51 Martin, Roger, *The Design of Business*, Boston, Harvard Business Press, 2009.

52 Adams, James L., *op. cit.*

for new ideas. He also reviews Alex Osborn's concept of brainstorming, with its suspension of judgment, and William J.J. Gordon's "synectics" approach using four types of analogies.

Tom Kelley

Tom Kelley[53] identifies a checklist of five paired barriers and bridges to creativity developed at IDEO. These pairs (with the barrier listed first) include:

- Hierarchy-Based/Merit-Based
- Bureaucracy/Autonomy
- Anonymous/Familiar
- Clean/Messy
- Experts/Tinkerers

IDEO is always worth examining because in addition to producing many high-performance design products, it has, more than any other design firm, consciously developed and tested many approaches and heuristics in the design process and used them to improve their results.

Teresa M. Amabile

Creativity in Context[54] is Amabile's update to her earlier work, *The Social Psychology of Creativity,* in which she formulates a theoretical framework for the social psychology of creativity based on her own and others' field research. There are a number of useful principles in this very scholarly work.

"Intrinsic motivation is conducive to creativity, but extrinsic motivation is detrimental," Amabile writes. This statement is in the original publication and is softened slightly by some exceptions in the update. This is significant for professional designers who earn their living by extrinsic reward (financial compensation) for their creativity. In my experience, it is generally true of creative people that extrinsic financial reward is lower on the list of motivators than many things, but (extrinsic) peer recognition tends to be high on the list for most.

[53] Kelley, Tom, *op. cit.*, p. 180-181.

[54] Amabile, *op. cit.*

Amabile's work to define criteria for creativity draws on an interesting paper by Jackson and Messick[55] in which they suggest that judgments of outstanding creativity are composed of four aesthetic responses occurring together: "surprise (unusualness), satisfaction (appropriateness), stimulation (transformation) and savoring (condensation, summary, simplicity or Less is more?)." These seem to me to be pretty concise criteria for a high-performance design.

Her theoretical framework of creative performance contains three components:

- Domain relevant skills (domain knowledge, skill, talent)
- Creativity relevant skills (cognitive style, knowledge of heuristics)
- Task motivation (attitude).

These components seem to be relevant (even if obvious) and therefore useful reminders about requirements for team success.

She has a very useful chart of positive and negative, general and organizational influences on creativity. Examples include optimal challenge (general, positive), co-worker skill diversity (organizational, positive), surveillance (general, negative), and win-lose competition within the organization (organizational, negative).

Carl R. Rogers

Psychologist Carl Rogers offers two interesting "conditions fostering constructive creativity."[56] One is "psychological safety" through acceptance of unconditional individual worth, absence of external evaluation, and empathetic understanding. The other is "psychological freedom," of symbolic expression, to be one's self to think, and to be responsible.

Summary

There are doubtless other published explorations of creativity that can add ideas on stimulating performance. Any ideas need to be assessed in the

55 Jackson, P. and S. Messick, "The person, the product and the response: Conceptual problems in the assessment of creativity," Journal of Personality, 1965, p. 33, 309-329.

56 Rogers, Carl R., "Toward a Theory of Creativity" essay in Creativity and its Cultivation, ed. Anderson, Harold H., New York, Harper & Row 1959, p. 69-82.

context of the teams that might benefit from them. It is likely that there will be resistance and skepticism about influences on creative performance, but without the curiosity and willingness to try, the potential for improvement has no chance.

There are no answers here, only experiences and ideas that may provide tools for your discovery and design of an appropriate high pH environment.

DELIVERY AND IMPLEMENTATION

It is easy as a student designer to believe that design is a worthy end in itself. In many cases, the recognition given to unrealized designs by peers who have been influenced in some way by them can be a satisfying reward for a designer and certainly can add to the thought stream that influences future realized work.

But ultimately the purpose of design is to produce an outcome that has a direct and positive impact on the real world. The realization of a design is essential to that purpose. James L. Adams refers to this as "the critical aspect of coaxing the idea into reality."

However, the methods used to realize most building design in the past half century have been demonstrated to be both error-prone and extremely wasteful of resources. Estimates of that waste are in the broad range of 30 percent to 60 percent. Designers must take responsibility to realize design more effectively than this. An obligation that goes with our capabilities and our privileged position as anointed professionals in society is to fix what is wrong with the way we deliver our services and artifacts (the mantras of "Heal thyself" and "Do no harm" come to mind). The savings produced by eliminating that waste alone could finance much of the planet and society's critical needs.[57]

Sustainable design must account for the entire process of implementation, not just for appropriate use of materials and systems and recycling of waste. The most hopeful approach to improving this is through integrating design and delivery, eliminating the gulf between them into which so much valuable information and understanding of intent is lost.

---

[57] Thirty percent of annual U.S. construction alone is more than $250 billion. The World Bank's estimate of the amount required to raise all the world's poorest to a basic needs level is $124 billion. (Sachs, *The End of Poverty*, Penguin, New York, 2005, p. 290.)

PROCESS

Why is process an issue for high-performance design? you might ask. Isn't design best left as an intuition-based exploration that determines its own direction based on the ideas discovered? It is true that design is not linear but rather an iterative process that seeks to close in on a best solution through developing (ideating), comparing, testing, and mutating possibilities. Nonetheless, there are common issues that always must be considered to achieve a relevant solution. Further, without a prioritized process, it is easy to spend a profligate amount of time on interesting aspects of a design that have little relevance to its ultimate purpose. This is not a comment about the big idea versus a detail of execution. The latter can be just as essential to the final reality as the former.

But designers can fall in love with ideas regardless of their relevance and can find great comfort in developing and refining peripheral ideas at the expense of a focused pursuit of the issues at hand. It is much like the person who searches for a lost piece of jewelry under the streetlamp, not because that is where it was lost but because the light is better there.

Because design is not linear, it is not improved by industrial improvement methodologies such as the Toyota Production System, which has great success in establishing an ideal culture for improvement in repetitive work but is not very useful for the messy exploration that is the creative process. The most efficient production processes are those that can be standardized, repeated, and refined down to total elimination of any wasted motion. In a nonlinear creative process, that ideal works against achieving the best possible solution, which is found through iterative ideation, modeling, and testing, the result of which determines direction. On the other hand, creativity can be subject to process improvement that recognizes its specific character. The Toyota Product Development[58] approach has much to offer in this regard. One of the interesting aspects of that is set-based concurrent design, which minimizes the early elimination of options on project components; rather, it concurrently develops those options until "the last responsible moment" when a choice must be made. This allows a wider range of edge-stretching options to be considered while still ensuring cost and schedule safety by including safe or proven options within the range. Other interesting aspects of the approach are rigorous capture of learning and extensive use of prototyping.

---

58 See Kennedy, Michael N., *Product Development for the Lean Enterprise*, Richmond, Va.: Oaklea Press, 2003.

At the macro scale, some of the basic tools and steps can be standardized in pursuing project definition, discovery of influences and possibilities, and even ideation without hindering the iterative approach. The art of process for design is in achieving the best balance that produces results within the limits of committable resources.

Tom Kelley, in his book about the design firm IDEO, says that their "'secret formula' is actually not very formulaic. It's a blend of methodologies, work practices, culture and infrastructure. Methodology alone is not enough."[59]

TOOLS/HEURISTICS

The tools that I want to emphasize here are not the digital tools of modeling and analysis, as important as those are. Those tools are rapidly changing, and their appropriate and effective use is an ongoing balancing act of high art. The most important thing I can say about that type of tool is that a high pH firm needs to stay alert to opportunities for new tools, try those that look promising in a meaningful way, and adopt them at the time they can clearly deliver an affordable advantage to the firm's purpose. A way to stay aware, aside from expecting IT support staff to keep the firm advised, is to encourage curiosity in this arena and enable experimentation by passionate advocates. The cost of this is manageable, and the buzz and energy it creates is a part of pushing creativity.

What I do want to focus on here are heuristics or techniques to assist in discovery of purpose and influences, tools to stimulate ideation, and tools to optimize process.

Charrette. All of the American design firms I am familiar with commonly use a process of design exploration that we all call a "charrette," a group effort to develop or refine problem definition, concepts, or details. European designers do essentially the same thing but are more likely to call it a workshop process. This has become a tightly ingrained part of the typical design process. But the effectiveness of it varies wildly depending on leadership, planning, focus, talent, and the heuristics used to stimulate ideas. For high design performance, this must be a rigorously driven process in which humor is often a key stimulant and techniques to stimulate creativity are engaged.

Parallel team pursuit. Having two or more teams develop concepts indepen-

[59] Kelley, Tom, *op. cit.* p.

dently and simultaneously leads to multiple possibilities, and iterations of this usually yield a rich set.

Heuristics. A couple of heuristics (exploratory problem-solving techniques) often tried (and sometimes imbedded within charrettes) include:

Brainstorming

Originally described by Alex Osborn and characterized by prohibition of evaluation as ideas are developed, it has lost its caché for many. But Tom Kelley describes "seven secrets for better brainstorming" developed by IDEO:[60]

- Sharpen the focus (edgy not fuzzy)
- Playful rules (deflect critique)
- Number ideas (go for quantity)
- Build and jump (push to either expand a topic or jump to a new one)
- The space remembers (make use of spatial/visual organization)
- Stretch your mental muscles (use a warm-up technique)
- Get physical (use physical objects).

IDEO has a strong reputation for effective ideation, and anyone who has experienced an ideation session with them has likely been energized by it.

Other possibilities for useful heuristics follow.

Dr. Edward De Bono's[61] approaches to breaking the tyranny of left-brain, vertical, logical, sequential thinking may be helpful to free the creativity of particularly constipated teams. This may be especially applicable when attempting design collaboration with inexperienced team members (builders, fabricators, and users come to mind).

De Bono's several books on lateral thinking include techniques for reducing the dominance of pre-set ideas, for relaxing, and for forcing changes in perspective.

60 Kelley, *op. cit.*, p.56-62.

61 De Bono, Edward, *Lateral Thinking: Creativity Step by Step,* New York, Harper & Row 1970.
De Bono's Thinking Course, New York, Facts On File, 1982.
New Think, New York, Avon Books 1967.
Six Thinking Hats, Boston, Little Brown & Co 1985.

Roger Von Oech[62] has an amusing and visual way of presenting a series of heuristics covering discovery, definition, and delivery as well as ideation. This will test the sense of humor of a design team, and the more erudite members may choke on some of its childlike (they may see childish) nature.

William J.J. Gordon's book on synectics[63] includes stimulating ways to use four types of analogy: personal (you as object), direct (domain transfer), symbolic (imagery based), and fantasy (wishful).

In his book *Brain Rules: 12 Principles for Surviving and Thinking at Work, Home and School,*[64] molecular biologist John Medina provides a great set of principles about how our brains work that are useful in designing the way design teams might work. It includes advice about differences in sleep needs for different people (suggesting one way we might organize teams), about the impact of lack of control on stress and therefore on health, the advantages of multi-sensory stimulation, and the ability to continue improving our brains through continued curiosity. One simple clue he offers: sleep on it after you have the data but before you start to ideate.

Dr. Atul Gawande is a curious surgeon at Brigham and Women's Hospital in Boston. In his search to become a better surgeon, he has researched how best to deal with complexity and concludes in his book *The Checklist Manifesto: How to Get Things Right*[65] that a well constructed and culturally implemented checklist is one of the most effective tools to achieve excellence in anything complex — from flying airplanes to surgery to building high rises.

I mention Daniel J. Levitin's[66] work (on the neuropsychology of music) not specifically on the basis of heuristics, though his advice that music is a more effective communicator of feeling and emotion than language might cause you to use music more to stimulate creativity. I include it mostly because it is indicative of the kind of work that can inspire us to think differently. Among other things, he discusses the existence of mirror neurons, which affect the way we learn physical actions through observation. What can we do with that?

---

62 Von Oech, Roger, A Kick in the Seat of the Pants, New York, Harper & Row 1986.
A Whack on the Side of the Head, New York, US Game Systems, Inc. 1983.

63 Gordon,W, *Synectics: The Development of Creative Capacity*, New York, Harper & Row, 1961.

64 Medina, John, *Seattle*, Pear Press, 2008.

65 Gawande, Atul, *op. cit.*

66 Levitin, Daniel J., T*his Is Your Brain on Music: The Science of a Human Obsession*, New York Penguin Group, 2006

Perhaps some of the best known and successful heuristics were used by Kenya Hara in setting up three exhibitions: The Architects Macaroni Exhibit (1995), the RE-Design Exhibition (2000), and the HAPTIC Exhibition (2004). In each case, the heuristic is inherent in the exhibit title: design it in macaroni, redesign the common commodities, and design to awaken all senses. In Kenya's words, the latter pursues the question: "A watering mouth is a taste response to sizzling meat. What kind of design can induce the reaction of a watering mouth from all five senses?"[67] And these heuristics inspired the Wave-Ripple, Loop, Surf pastas of Tadusu Ohe, the square toilet paper roll of Shigeru Ban, and the Kami Tama hair lamp of Kosuke Tsumura (and many others) respectively.

This brief synopsis of some of the work on heuristics is intended only to suggest that there is a continuous body of work being created that can benefit the quest for higher performance in design and should be routinely visited. When you think that you have perfected the approach to ideation is probably when you most need to be forced into an alternate perspective.

[67] Hara, Kenya, *op. cit.*, p. 83.

Projects at NBBJ

We spent a lot of time doing projects that were designer-led, project-manager driven, technical-architect documented, and construction-administrator implemented. In simpler times, with simpler projects, and with modest aspirations this produced acceptable results. But it could not achieve a high-performance design.

We evolved by trial and error and in fits and starts as we tried various modifications in the way we went about our projects. Things we tried were influenced by ideas brought to us from other firms, ideas we discovered from other industries, and things we ideated internally. This evolution has led us to the current state described below, but which is continuously being challenged and tweaked.

Definition and Discovery

Discovery evolved at NBBJ from focusing on thorough team understanding of the client's program ("brief" in Europe) including time and cost implications, site influences, and regulatory and political requirements and precedents, to include a much broader social, political, technological, and enterprise-aspiration based process.

To enable this, our specialists in behavior, economics, and specific building types are heavily involved. The behaviorist group, REV, uses a number of techniques to help clients and users discover and articulate future possibilities.

In the design competition for Reebok Headquarters, the team reviewed the entire history of the company, its annual reports, all of their brand messages, and specifically the words of CEO Paul Fireman describing his aspirations: "I don't want an office building. I want a place that is the spirit of innovation … . Our mission is to revitalize and refocus our identity, to energize our work force and launch a new, highly productive and innovation-based future." From that the design team gleaned a desire to transform the company completely by getting the product design and marketing staff to live and breathe the essence of the company's recreational footwear products. This led to the concept of multiple sports and recreation venues interlocked with the headquarters functions to immerse staff in the use and testing of their products. That concept won the competition. After moving into this new headquarters in 2000, Reebok's product time to market was significantly reduced, and the company had five straight years of earnings improvements. In 2004, sales increased 9 percent and earnings per share grew by 26 percent over the prior year. During this five-year period, Reebok's share price increased more than 400 percent, and it has outperformed the S&P 500 every year. The company was recently acquired by Adidas AG.

A lesson learned about the importance and character of cost analysis during discovery, which is the goal- and expectation-setting stage of a project, came from collaboration with Cesar Pelli on the physics building at the University of Washington. Our rigorous and conscientious process designer on the project was about to present a detailed analysis of project cost at an early pre-design meeting. Pelli, who through a failure in our collaboration had not seen the estimate, insisted that he must review it first. He promptly identified a number of areas where he declared the costs were setting expectations below the design aspirations and insisted on dramatic increases in those areas. He is right: All expectation setting should fully address the project's aspirations. That doesn't mean that the balance between aspiration and means is not part of an ongoing performance design process, but it does mean that they must be on the table early and openly.

The discovery process for our Alaska Native Medical Center included the principal designer (Richard Dallam) spending several weeks in a number of native Alaska settlements getting to know how people lived and what they valued. Without that experience, we would not have learned how to communicate effectively with their elders (from a lower eye level and with emphasis on physical demonstration) and certainly would not have been able to isolate common themes cutting through these diverse cultures (e.g., circle of life and distance perception through hue).

To explore clients' culture and image expectations, we sometimes used image selection and collage techniques (having them select images and create a collage expressing what they felt success would feel like), both as individual and team exercises with the client. At San Diego Children's Hospital and a number of other places, we used a large archive of local current and historic photographs with board, staff, and patients to get a sense of what they related to as quintessentially San Diegan. We used that in taking our first pass at creating form that might seem familiar and friendly to young San Diego patients.

We develop project stories with clients, sometimes specific about staff and customer experiences, such as the walk from the entrance to the pharmacy in a retail drugstore; sometimes about enterprise aspirations, such as changing the way staff perceive their mission; but always with the intent to define desired outcome.

In doing this kind of intensive pre-design exploration, we have learned that regardless of how essential it seems to high-performance outcome, it must be done in a very affordable way. This is especially sensitive relative to client and user time commitment. As eager as a high-performance design client may seem for transformation, they will often be shocked by the time that the process can consume, and part of high performance is to protect them from that over-commitment.

Ideation

When I entered the practice, our approach to ideation was a simple process of a designer supported by a few assistants (usually less experienced designers) confronting and overcoming a blank sheet based on the clients' program and a little dialogue. It evolved a lot as we continued to learn more about what design is for, how to understand clients better, how to help clients understand and articulate their aspirations, what obstacles get in the way of delivering design, and how teams can work more creatively.

Our initial studio experiment resulted in a studio culture based on the concept that the entire project team must be a part of the ideation process (and "own" the result) if they were to carry out the design effectively. Based on the immediate improvement we saw from that model in the quality of the executed design, we widely adopted that approach. It brought broader and new perspectives to the table. The issue then was how to draw everyone into the process effectively and increase both the quantity and quality of ideas. To make that happen, our charrette processes had to be led by effective designers willing to engage people and help in the articulation of their ideas and lead the effort of editing, mutating, and selecting the best. It took time to get designers to see the benefit and then gain comfort with the role.

Individuals find stimulation in different approaches .We developed sub-team approaches to focus on different aspects of the problem in series with the object of discovering what breakthroughs the different perspectives might generate. We have had each team member develop abstract precept physical models, using form, material, texture, color, and occasionally sound or smell to convey the essence of key aspects of a project concept. These have been effective in loosening form preconceptions but not always. Some teams have felt it was too abstract and a waste of time. Lesson learned? Let teams tailor their own processes, but have leaders ensure that they are stretching.

We typically develop and pursue a number of concepts in parallel through several stages of ideation, critiquing and then altering team composition at each stage.

This usually has had the effect of strengthening initial concepts and providing a richer concept base, as well as giving all participants a stronger sense of influence over the outcome.

We developed stories, demonstrated by concepts, about what the expected experience would be, and like many designers we used a lot of analogy. Gordon Walker, when he was a principal at NBBJ, added a useful litmus test on the reality of verbal tools. It was used primarily as a critique comment: "Sounds good ... looks bad!" This often caused a worthwhile rethink.

We developed approaches to drawing users into the design process, mostly, at first, at the plan development stage. This was done largely through gaming to help them understand the interrelatedness of plan decisions. Then we could explore the three-dimensional aspects of those decisions with them as we gained their trust and helped them understand the impact of form. Through this process, users would often adopt a broader and less personally focused set of priorities about design. On the other hand, I gamed with a hospital emergency department staff for an entire afternoon trying to develop alternatives, but one very determined participant would push everything back to the same idea time after time (until my choices were either giving up or administering a hearty head slap).

Physical modeling plays a key role in the design process, from very small-scale building models (often dozens of 3-D printed models) to very large-scale models of portions of the building. One team working on the detailed development of the Reebok project took a page from Toyota's book when they were having a tough time detailing the atrium wall. They pulled the plug on all other parts of the project and focused the entire design team for a week on building a very large-scale model of the wall to solve the troublesome details.

When a concept direction is established, we often develop project posters for the team space to provide a continuous touch point and remind us and the client of what the important concept drivers are, and to keep the detailed development focused on those ideas.

Project Delivery/Implementation

We were in the fortunate position in the early decades of the firm of doing the majority of our work with a small group of skilled and conscientious builders in the Northwest. We had great working relationships most of the time, and our skills in cost control were a helpful tool in keeping it that way. In more recent times, we have worked with a much broader range of builders with a more diverse set of characteristics, some of them less charming.

Our best results in terms of design delivered have always come when there has been mutual respect and a success-focused attitude on the part of owner, designer, and builder. Not so amazing.

Much of that happened with either long-time builder collaborators or trusted advisor relationships with clients. Our Columbus, Ohio, office successfully took on a handful of designer-led (at-risk) design-build projects, all health care related. Partners Friedl Bohm and Doug Parris structured and led these efforts.

With the advent of building information modeling (BIM), which we took on in 1997 through Bentley's tool sets, we began to see the potential for broader designer-builder collaboration. We were working at that too slowly when we had a serious wake-up call. In 2004, Scott Wyatt and I were invited by David Mortenson to visit his firm's Disney Hall project in its last days of construction. We spent a day with their team in Los Angeles reviewing the building but more enlightening than that, reviewing the process they used to get it built. When we boarded the flight back to Seattle that evening we were both elated and devastated. Elated that a much better way of building had been demonstrated as eminently feasible and our belief in BIM reinforced, but devastated that as hard as we thought we had pushed, we were behind a builder in pushing the envelope. Behind a builder!

We felt strongly that there was an opportunity to take a paradigm-shifting leap in project delivery right in front of us. We brought the Mortenson team to a principals retreat shortly after that to raise firm awareness. And shortly after that we restructured the firm core team to add a managing partner for delivery. (At that point, the firm core team had been three managing partners: for design, for practice, and for markets.) We began an accelerated program to push BIM as a tool and integrated project delivery (IPD) as a process. We did a lot of learning and teaching inside the firm as well as setting and pursuing goals for implementation. We did a lot of aggressive information sharing with potential collaborators outside the firm (builders, fabricators, consultants, and clients). We signed one of the first big hospital project integrated delivery contracts (Palo Alto Medical Center using Sutter Health's version of IPD), and we developed our own model IPD contract, which is more BIM savvy. We recently completed a health care project in the Seattle area under an IPD agreement led by managing partner Jay Halleran. While the economic crash has retarded the spread of IPD a bit, in the long run, I believe it will become the contract and process of choice for clients seeking high-performance design. The next step beyond that is the true total performance value-based approach, with bigger risk and reward sharing that is still reasonable and manageable for high pH firms.

NBBJ has recently pioneered large segment prefabrication (combined patient room headwall and bathrooms) and has used off-the-shelf jet bridges for both temporary and permanent connections in a health care project.

Process Design

At NBBJ in the 1990s, we stumbled across the benefits of an approach that we came to call "process design" — a term we have since seen widely used. We came on this approach through the mother of invention (necessity) when we won a project with a seemingly impossible schedule, a very tight design and construction budget, a client with high design expectations, and our own expectations of high performance. Our approach at the time was to have an experienced project manager develop a project plan and schedule to use in negotiations with our engineering consultants, and share it with the design team. The first pass of that on this project suggested convincingly that we could not succeed. We gathered the team to seek ideas on how we could minimize our losses.

But someone at that session said this was nonsense (or words to that effect) and insisted that we take a shot at reinventing the way we go about the project, designing a pathway that would meet all project goals. The team was enthusiastic to go for it and began a process of designing a new and tailored approach, which took the first two weeks of a five and a half month schedule to accomplish. They reconsidered all of our usual assumptions about roles, interrelationships, phases, drawing scales … virtually everything. They eliminated phase reviews in favor of weekly interactive document and issue collaboration, accelerated key design decisions that cut across disciplines, and changed traditional scales on many documents to reduce the total produced within readable tolerances. The result was an agreed process plan that would deliver the project, meeting all of its goals and expectations. Most important, it was developed and committed to by all of the people who had to make it happen — client, architect, and engineers. This was a government-sponsored project, which at the time had to be hard bid, so builders could not be a part of the process. The process plan included means of communication, constant mutual feedback on progress, and the means for continuous correction to accommodate the aberrations of a nonlinear reality. It was our first use of a visual dynamic calendar as a planning, negotiating, tracking, and management tool. The end result of the project was that it did meet or exceed all of the expectations (including financial success for the client and for the designers, and a design award and publication for the project). It was several hundred thousand gross square feet, delivered from the starting gun to hard bid date in the above mentioned five and a half months. And very, very important, it resulted in high morale, pride and sense of accomplishment for the design team.

This was eye-opening, and we quickly began refining and teaching this process design approach to all of our studios and design teams and developed tools to aid the process, including digital tools to help geographically dispersed teams.

Effective process design incorporates enlightened lean strategies:

- Tailored project plan (process design, designed and owned by stakeholders)
- Rigorous capture of learning (precedent analysis, prior learning)
- Set based concurrent designs (rapid ideation, bracket multiple options for analysis)
- Iterative spiral approach (from *Product Development for the Lean Enterprise*, by Michael Kennedy.)

The goal of process design is to design the best way to achieve our projects goals by focusing our effort where it can be most effective. Key process design tools include:

- Dynamic calendar
- Client decision plan
- Project goals and schedules
- Modeled products
- Communication plan
- Team meeting set agenda
- Team organizational diagrams, roles, and responsibilities.

Tools/Heuristics

Soon after I became CEO in 1983, I became interested in exploring means to increase the creative stimulus in the firm. I reviewed the work of creativity experts such as von Oech, DeBono, and James L. Adams and pushed on the teams I worked with to try some of their thinking techniques to generate a wider range and specifically new sets of alternatives. Indeed, I was so enthusiastic that I used a Christmas celebration luncheon for firm leaders to lecture on De Bono's "six thinking hats" idea. Yes, I lectured rather than discussed, and I even wore a special derby hat for the occasion (it was white, De Bono's color for facts, figures, and other objective information). At a Christmas celebration it was as inappropriate as it was unwelcomed, but it did get across the point that we had to push harder at ideation. I went on to teach a class in the firm about ways to use these heuristic tools with design teams. Probably the primary benefit of this effort was to send a very readable signal that we needed to raise the bar for our design solutions rather than creating any direct process improvement.

Later we picked up on the work of IDEO, made several site visits to learn from them, and included them in several prospect efforts. Out of that familiarization we picked up on their use of the "card deck" of creative heuristics that, among other things, allows a team to shift the focus of an ideation session quickly and re-energize it when it is bogging down. We also picked up on the power of their "tech-box" full of interesting stuff. Our offices have had more interesting stuff on hand ever since.

A prospect team pursuing a children's hospital that I led included IDEO on our team and went through a two-day deep dive with them in their San Francisco office. It was energizing and informative, and I learned that big fat handles on tooth brushes are great for little kids. The direct approach of observing teenagers at local schools broadened our way of seeing. That experience had a more direct impact on our project approach and indirectly led to our forming a behavioral based group we named REV.

When chaos theory was a hot topic in the early 1990s, we were drawn by the beauty of some of the imagery but more usefully by the notion of self-similarity at multiple scales, which became a bit of a heuristic in development of detail in support of concept.

We also admired and adopted ideas from Jerry Hirschberg's book, (and I tried unsuccessfully to get him to join our board).

Like most firms, we use design charrettes to generate ideas, and we design those charrettes specifically for the stage the project is in and the cast of stakeholders involved. We decided to err on the side of inclusiveness in these charrettes because we feel that the benefit of diverse thinking is worth the cost of management/leadership energy that it takes to stay productive. In a conversation with Bjarke

Ingels about the degree of inclusiveness in his design processes (which is high) he said that he did not agree with an approach taken by some who feel that the sole purpose of ideation is to elicit a large quantity of ideas, and that "any lame idea is worthwhile." I generally agree that a lot of ideas that have no apparent relevance are not affordable in a time management perspective, but some seemingly irrelevant ideas trigger connections that cause a breakthrough. At least part of design exploration needs to be wide ranging. Another truth is that a good idea doesn't care where it came from, a notion that was a mantra for my partner Scott Wyatt and which we took seriously at NBBJ.

We internally developed a few digital tools that are helpful in effective implementation, among them the "digital dynamic dalendar" mentioned earlier, which supports process design and was created by Steve McConnell and Alex Maxim. This provides a digital framework for process design and coordination, which also prompts a big-picture understanding of what the project strategy and tactics are at every point along the way. We developed a complete set of construction administration tools compatible with the major systems (primarily Prologue) in use by contractors, created by Dave Leptich. Internal development of digital tools is risky, expensive, and time consuming but worthwhile when they uniquely support effective ways of working, and in these cases the investment paid off. On the other hand, we attempted several times to develop programming tools for healthcare and never created a viable solution because we couldn't reach a manageable focus.

I mentioned our group, REV, above, which has done remarkable work for some of our clients in translating their brand into graphic, color, and image reality. When working with architectural teams, we use them most extensively in the discovery and project definition stage, where they have skills and techniques to help our clients and users explore and express their needs, goals, and dreams. This adds a dimension to our understanding on projects, but we still are working on the difficulty in translating the behaviorist language into relevant form. This collaboration is important to get right.

Certainly the big tool question for architectural designers in recent years has been the digital project support suite. We jumped into CAD in 1983 (with Sigma Design), coinciding with the first studio experience and a giant health care project. That new studio team, headed by Dennis Forsyth and Pat James, did the remarkable in creating a new culture, implementing and debugging a new CAD system, designing an award-winning major medical center, and being financially successful. It was a high-risk, high-reward approach that succeeded. We followed that CAD system for a number of years until it was clear that it would not to be the industry winner. Then looking ahead to 3-D BIM (object-based design, in Bentley language), we were an early adopter of that approach in the late 1990s. We struggled to unify the firm under one tool set for several years until we recognized that that was not likely to happen in the industry for some time, if ever. We pushed to have a primary system but enabled experimentation. We followed developments in a number of systems both for mainstream BIM and for model integration and in 2005 began to let Revit take over as mainstream for us, but we still worked with stronger programs for things like parametric design and model integration. And more recently, as Autodesk acquired either these capabilities or in some cases the companies that created them, the firm has basically switched to the Revit suite. However, a lesson learned is that in spite of the advantages of uniformity in platform (support costs, ease of cross-studio projects, etc.), well considered exceptions are essential to staying near the edge of possibilities.

We experimented early with parametric design, which at first simply produced interesting forms and then rationalized them for construction. More recently we are discovering ways to set parameters that answer key performance issues, and most of this discovery is coming from supporting curious staff's efforts.

Projects in Danish Firms

Most Danish design firms get the majority of their work from design competitions (mostly invited or prequalified variety) and that was true of these six. They all have competition-focused teams, often supplemented by specialists appropriate to the building type. They all ensure follow-through on their projects by some members of the competition team staying with the project for some period beyond the competition stage. This means, though, that for the most part they are not getting start-to-finish project involvement of the majority of their teams. The exception to this is the youngest practice, **BIG**, which seems to engage pretty much its whole team at some level start to finish.

3XN has each project team headed by two partners, one of whom is considered backup. **Schmidt Hammer Lassen** has all teams led by a partner or associate partner.

I found the team discontinuity from competition through occupancy disappointing but not surprising in a design-competition-driven environment.

Definition and Discovery

It is not clear how the discovery process has evolved in these firms. They generally describe discovery as an important aspect of their work, but they do not articulate a specific approach to it.

3XN describes its approach as based on an understanding of "the context in which we build—the physical surroundings as well as the social, cultural, and historical context in general" and describes its process as investigating the site and asking people questions to "find the story the building should tell." But it is not specific about methodology. It does, however, have a group, **GXN**, which focuses on incorporating technological possibilities in the work.

Arkitema is the most articulate in talking about its discovery process through "implementing user analyses, user consultation, user-driven innovation, and process facilitation ... to include social and cultural dimensions." They focus on peoples' lives (behavioral observation) rather than asking users directly in exploring potential, challenges, and issues. They specifically seek unrecognized needs, those that users are either unaware of or unable to articulate.

BIG has the attitude that any difficult project can be redefined in terms of its possibilities as a means to find the breakthrough solution. It uses storytelling to help a building come into being but thinks of those stories as being about the project's birth not its future life. The building's life after that is a dialogue between it and the world.

C.F. Moller has a discovery approach that demands the development of a complete project story before starting physical explorations. They feel that this ensures a commonly understood project footing for both client and designer. They have occasionally brought in outsiders to broaden their perspectives (e.g., Texas A&M's Roger Ulrich in health care).

Henning Larsen has three doctoral students helping to discover sustainable possibilities in their work as part of the discovery and implementation process. They have worked with outside experts (from the Danish Experimentarium) to draw out relevant directions when the program given had lofty but vague goals, such as the Syrian Cultural Center in Damascus. They also have used a consultant (on cultural innovation) to facilitate user/designer dialogue in defining goals and success measures.

Schmidt Hammer Lassen has used outsiders in theater, library, and courts to open their exploratory perspective. The firm's teams seek to establish an iconic set of word descriptors in the discovery process, which become touchstones for design.
Ideation in Danish Firms

Bjarke Ingels was alone among the firm leaders with whom I talked in having looked at the work of creative theorists, and as I indicated earlier, he specifically reacted against the notion pushed in "workshop zoos" that "the lame idea and the good idea have equal value." He has established that you get great ideas in an environment that is fun, collaborative, and neither fear- nor competition-based.

But all of these firms seemed intuitively to value and encourage diversity of viewpoint in the ideation process.

3XN describes its ideation as workshop-centered, with partners, users, and various experts all part of it. They work heavily with physical (cardboard, largely) models.

Arkitema emphasizes "co-design" with users, where the design process is very interactive in a real-time sense.

BIG is about a hypothetical deductive method of hypothesis, trial, test, and confirm or reformulate the hypothesis. It uses a Darwinian formulation of excess (ideas) and selection, where, as in nature, the selection is not for the strongest, fastest, or smartest but for the most adaptable (accommodating). Thus the mantra "Yes is more."

C.F.Moller involves everyone in the pursuit of common architectural goal rooted in shared philosophy. That philosophy is rooted in a Nordic tradition of craftsmanship, simplicity, clarity, and unpretentious solutions for people, place, and function.

Henning Larsen talks of tailoring "the working method in relation to the specific project," and its exploration is underlain by the search to find ways to "change the world."

Schmidt Hammer Lassen describes a process of a ping-pong of ideas, with time between to digest what went before and clear establishment of the project idea before creating form. The process uses workshops with the entire team to come to common understanding.

Delivery/Implementation

The majority of projects by these firms are procured by competitive tender, but public-private partnership in a design-build-operate-finance format has recently gained ground, and in that case has created closer builder/designer collaboration. None of these firms seems near the front edge of integrated delivery, though **Arkitema** is rigorously pursuing BIM as an enabler, has a history of exploring project delivery improvement, and has an entity called Arkitema Prefab, which has "constructed prefabricated elements for everything from window systems and banister types to whole single-family houses." Perhaps because all of the five founding partners were carpenters at one time, the firm has been a leader in designing from a constructability perspective.

Process

I did not discover a particularly well articulated process approach in any of these six firms. Naturally enough, all seem to follow an accelerated process of discovery and ideation during design competitions, but none except BIG articulated a very specific commitment to a process or to process design. BIG's process of excess ideas and Darwinian mutation is only part of a total process of design and delivery. I think that they all have default processes that they rely on that have been effective in their success, and perhaps they consciously adjust (optimize) those for specific projects. I also think that they all could experience a leap forward by spending the time to more consciously design (and refine) their process approach, specifically by doing some version of process design for each project.

Tools/Heuristics

Of these firms, only two talked of specific heuristic devices in their approach: **Arkitema** alludes to them in its "Arkitema sensemaking" process, and uses plasticine figures handcrafted by staff to reinforce that people are their starting place and at the same time reinforcing the role that humor plays in the process. They also emphasize their adoption of BIM and its use to aid construction.

Schmidt Hammer Lassen uses "value words," which, as earlier described, define the essential nature or DNA of the project.

I was not surprised at the limited use of heuristics because, in my knowledge of many architectural design firms, I know of almost none who has experimented with them, in spite of the evidence of success from product and industrial design firms.

PROJECTS

The projects shown here, by both NBBJ and the Danish firms described in this book, have received significant peer recognition through design competitions, publications, or design awards, and in many cases through all three. In addition, they contribute significantly to the mission performance of their sponsors and were achieved with a relative economy of means, thereby achieving most aspects of high-performance design.

Rendering courtesy of Henning Larsen Architects

Massar Children's Discovery Centre
Damascus
Henning Larsen Architects

This project is the heart of a Syrian educational program — Massar — located in the center of Damascus. The center offers exhibitions and hands-on experiences empowering young Syrians to contribute actively to building their future.

Inspired by the Syrian Damascus rose, the building is a framework for scientific and cultural exhibition. It includes exhibition, library, education, and administration space. The shell structure allows a playful, dazzling sceneography of light penetrating the interior spaces — like light filtering between rose petals. Exhibition and administrative areas are laid out between the petals creating interior labyrinth journeys inspired by walks in the old city of Damascus formed by walls with the sky as the window.

The center of the rose forms a large communal orientation space where people meet, share knowledge, and develop new ideas together — a cross pollination of knowledge. From here, journeys rise upwards in a web of ramps and steps interweaving the public plateau with the upper shell structure. The central vertical movement under the open sky challenges the traditional horizontal movement in the Arab city.

Rendering courtesy of Schmidt Hammer Lassen

The International Criminal Court The Hague, the Netherlands
The Hague, the Netherlands
Schmidt Hammer Lassen Architects

The new facility for the ICC encases the courts function, the tallest element in the complex, in a parterre garden utilizing plants from all 110 member nations. Justice delivered in a garden setting. The sunken garden entrance approach provides required security while encouraging trust, hope, and faith in the justice process.

Located close to the North Sea, the site is placed between nature and the city, connecting the dune landscape with the edge of the city. The compact buildings with small footprints return the landscape to the city so that the open spaces, the sky, and the horizon become an integrated part of the complex and its place in the city, communicating the values of the ICC.

Photos (clockwise from top) by Tim Griffith, Christian Richters, Dark Design

Telenor World Headquarters
Fornebue, Norway
NBBJ Architects

This project for Norway's telecommunications giant is a powerful expression of the company's vision to create the foremost creative working environment in Scandinavia — democratic, inspiring, and technologically advanced. The idea to consolidate up to 8,000 employees at 6,000 workstations accomplishes an open work plan on a grand scale. Now one of the largest free address workplaces in the world, the headquarters has successfully transformed the way the company conducts business. Signifying an investment in creativity, the project's democratic ideals and goals for innovation are rooted in a desire to enhance employee well being. The architecture not only provides inspiring new means for people to interact with technology and their surroundings but also establishes an environment of the highest aesthetic quality, focusing on three equally important issues: organizational flexibility, technology integration, and environmental sensitivity.

Photo by Adam Mørk

Ørestad College
Municipality of Copenhagen/Undervisnings — og Bygningsstyrelsen
3XN Architects

This upper secondary school provides an open framework for cross-discipline teaching and IT-based learning through a transformational classroom-free superstructure of four spatially interconnected levels.

Each level is a study zone, which enables organizational flexibility to create different learning environment spaces and group sizes.

The central stair openly connecting all levels and the roof terrace provides a unifying social interaction and viewing platforms. Each level includes an outdoor space contained within the overall superstructure connected from ground to roof.

The building won Best Building in Scandinavia in 2007.

"VM" and the Mountain
Orestad, Denmark
BIG-Bjarke Ingels Group architects

Photo by Jakob Galit

These two projects for the same developer transformed the notion of multifamily housing. The Mountain Dwellings takes the issue of providing a large car park serving the surrounding area and turns it into a hillside landscape for garden apartments terracing from the 11th floor to ground, each facing the sun. The roof gardens consist of a terrace and a garden with plants changing character according to the changing seasons. The building has a water-capturing system that maintains the roof gardens. The only thing that separates the apartment and the garden is a glass façade with sliding doors to provide light and fresh air.

Hangzhou Stadium
Hangzhou, China
NBBJ Architects with CCDI

Rendering courtesy of NBBJ

Like many cities in China, Hangzhou is undergoing rapid urban change shifting the city's expansion toward the Qian Tang riverfront. New construction has recently tripled the city's size, leaving an eclectic, hypermodern architectural fabric that is powerful in scale, yet nebulous in terms of public place making.

The Hangzhou Sports Park is a vibrant, pedestrian-centric recreation development located in the midst of Hangzhou's urbanization frenzy. Situated on the riverfront, the sports park is seen as an opportunity for creating lush, picturesque, and sustainable public spaces that are often elusive in the newly constructed context.

Drawing conceptually from the geometries of the nearby river delta, the flowing forms of the landscape planning are the principal means of organizing the site, defining circulation, and concentrating activities. The site is designed to create a seamless pedestrian experience that weaves together sports and commercial programs while forming a clear path of circulation between two major transportation hubs on the east and west ends of the site.

The site is composed of three layers of activity. An above-grade platform defines the "sports boulevard," which links together programs such as the main stadium and tennis tournament facilities. On the ground level, pathways, gardens, and plazas form a network of public recreation activities designed for alternative and extreme sports. Sunken spaces and courtyards lead to an extensive below-grade retail facility containing boutique stores, restaurants, and a multiplex cinema.

The primary architectural element on the site is the 80,000-seat stadium. The stadium's exterior geometry draws from the serene flora iconography found on the banks of Hangzhou's West Lake. The stadium bowl program, structure, and exterior shell create a unique concourse and circulation experience. On the north end of the stadium, the seating bowl opens up to reveal a view to the Yangtze riverfront and connect the sporting events to the city of Hangzhou.

Akershus University Hospital
C.F. Moller Architects

Photos by Torben Eskerod

This hospital in Oslo is one of Europe's best. It appears not as a traditional institutional building but as an informal and open place, integrating the daily lives of patients and families with the world outside. It makes patient stays as close to their normal life as possible. An internal skylit boulevard provides an orienting structure and incorporates such services as hairdresser, priest, library, café, and pharmacy, similar to a typical urban environment. Daylight and connection to the surrounding woodland play an important role in making the place feel welcoming and secure. It is highly sustainable, using locally sourced materials, and geothermal energy provides more than 40 percent of total energy consumption. It is the result of an international competition. Construction was completed on time and within budget. It won the U.K. Building Better Healthcare Award for Best International Design in 2009.

Photos courtesy of Arkitema

Sluseholman Community
Copenhagen
Arkitema Architects & Planners with Soeters Van Eldonk Ponec Architecten

This waterfront-focused residential district in Copenhagen's South Harbour has created an exceptional community balanced between a public side focused on harbor and canals and a more private side focused on generous and sunny courtyards. The courtyards provide both recreation and garden spaces. The organically diverse feel of the neighborhood was created by incorporating multiple individual architects designing individual dwellings within the shell structures and sensitive but flexible architectural guidelines.

Photo by Assassi Productions

Reebok World Headquarters
Canton, Massachusetts
NBBJ Architects

For this world headquarters project, architecture presented the means to re-focus and re-energize a company's work force and identity. Design goals were focused on energizing and inspiring the work force, building a cohesive and productive workplace, retaining and recruiting top talent from around the world, and enhancing the company's creative culture. A new type of workplace was created that connects all aspects of the business, bringing together the employees and their activities with the products and their intended uses. Certain components were considered essential to the company's health and fitness culture, such as physical activity, access to nature, daylight, fresh air, and childcare.

By integrating outdoor and indoor athletic activities and creating a transparent central spine to connect employee offices with the activities of Reebok's brand, the building provides a place where employees love to come to work and international visitors immediately connect with the Reebok brand. The design has helped bolster the company's productivity and improve product time to market. The project was achieved within Reebok's desired budget.

"Our mission was to revitalize and refocus the company's identity, to energize our work force, and launch a new, highly productive and innovation-based future. This meant providing a different environment. We wanted an inspiring and cohesive workplace that controls costs, promotes creativity, enhances the company's brand image, celebrates and expresses the company's culture, and serves to recruit and retain the industry's best talent," said Paul Fireman, former president/chairman/CEO of Reebok.

PRACTICE

Strategy, Development, Business Model

While the *raison d'être* of a high-performance design enterprise is projects, its continued existence both short term and long term is dependent on a practice or firm structure to sustain and guide its development. The practice must design strategy for accomplishing its vision and purpose, develop and implement that strategy, and create a business model that is consistent with its vision and purpose and effective in the marketplace.

The key to successful design of this structure for a high pH firm is clear focus on enabling design performance. In many firms, structure is modeled after non-creative entities and sometimes becomes self-justifying, bureaucratic, and even antagonistic to the messiness of the design process. That is a huge impediment to design performance.

As we look at each of these aspects of practice, it is a good time to restate what a high pH firm is.

A high pH firm:

- Consistently produces high-performance design
- Is inspiring for participants in the process
- Is both effective and efficient
- Is affordable to the user and society (in time and money)
- Is profitable to the design enterprise and financially equitable to the enterprise staff

STRATEGY

Enterprise strategy is the creative means for directing a practice future in dealing with the real world by:

- Knowing current client and social reality (unmet needs)
- Anticipating future possibilities

- Ideating the firm's desired place in that future
- Developing and committing to action

The process of periodically redeveloping strategy is also part of renewing commitment to values and purpose while updating them to currently understood realities.

Developing strategy requires a creative process of discovery, definition, and ideation to set a direction for the practice. The most important function of strategy is that it creates alignment and clarity in the firm's priorities for seeking and dealing with opportunities in projects, markets, personnel, and collaborations. This is critical because no matter how brilliant our plans are (remembering that the best way to make God laugh is to voice your plans for the future) they are dependent on opportunity. Although we can improve opportunity through rigorous pursuit, we are not likely to find everything we are looking for, and in the meantime, opportunities we weren't seeking will present themselves. High pH firms make strategic use of those opportunities through the insight of their strategy.

The development of strategy can and should happen at multiple levels of a practice, but this discussion focuses on the overall practice strategy. Strategy can be developed by any empowered creative group, but it is important in a high pH firm that the ultimate authors of the practice strategy have their professional and economic interests aligned with it (i.e., have the most at risk). The reason for this is that the strategy of a high pH firm must align with its values and purpose, which include both professional and economic aspects, and must be owned by those with the most power to implement it. Those who own the firm have the most power; those who do it have the most ownership of the purpose. They should be the same. There are a number of once-great firms that got this wrong.

Strategy should address the external issues of brand, marketing and sales, and firm citizenship (politically, socially, and philanthropically). Strategy must also address the internal issues of people, systems, and tools. And strategy must create a business model that spans external and internal impact.

Strategy can be as general as an articulation of intent and priority or it can be a very specific action plan. There are reams of advice by consultants on semantics (vision, mission, strategy, and tactics), methodology, inclusiveness, content, process, and follow through, and from time to time it can be informative to check them out, particularly to tailor the content and form of your strategy to your real needs.

In the best strategies for high performance, current prime competitors are usually not the major concern for the future. More likely it is the entrepreneurs operating at the edges of today's markets who will be key in defining future competition. They are the ones most likely to be looking intently for unmet needs and future directions.

A financial strategy goes hand in hand with the business model, which sets pricing and collections approach but is also specifically focused on providing firm stability, mainly dealing with ownership transition, profit distribution, and capitalization. To ensure financial stability, a firm should not highly leverage itself. High leveraging exposes the firm to high risk from many sources: interest rates, client failures, and economic downturn to name the easy ones. This means that owners will have high equity in the firm at all times and, yes, a lot of net worth at risk. Financially focused people may be tempted to make the firm's capital a profit center by seeking extraordinarily high return on that capital. That is another road to ruin as witnessed by Orange County California and Procter & Gamble, who both used highly leveraged derivatives to enhance profits and lost disastrously. Stick to design as your business as well as your profession.

A useful high-performance strategy starts with the firm's purpose and vision and ties it to actions to achieve them in the anticipated conditions of society, markets, and the globe. Both actions and anticipated conditions should be expressed as a bandwidth of possibilities broad enough to have a realistic chance of including future reality but narrow enough to provide significant guidance in action.

DEVELOPMENT

Development is to a large extent the action arm or the playing out of strategy. This aspect of practice is not usually front of mind for a designer, but it is an essential survival need of a high pH design entity.

Development implements firm strategies through the largely external issues of sales, marketing, public relations, branding, and philanthropy and through the largely internal issues of people development, systems, tools, and research.

Sales

For high design performance and for a high-performance design, the most important aspect of sales is the selection of prospects. The filter for selection of prospects must reflect the firm's purpose and values and be guided by its strategy. In the best of times, if a firm has a clearly established brand that reflects those values and purpose, it is relatively easy to be selective and true to its defined filter. The majority of real life, however, is not spent in the best of times, nor with an established brand that fully reflects performance aspirations. That is where the creative art of selection takes place. The issues are, Can a prospect become more aligned with our aspirations and benefit the client at the same time, and can we honestly sell that to the client during the selection process? And in the worst of times, What can we creatively do that will keep us moving forward, build rather than erode our brand, and provide performance that is particularly appropriate for the times? The filter should be strong and clear enough that these decisions can be made by the design team, not by any remote markets function.

Jerry Hirshberg recounts a time when NDI was asked to design a "global car," one whose appeal would cross all cultural boundaries.[68] Car designers apparently view this idea as shorthand for mass appeal that would offend (nor strongly attract) no one. In other words, this was an assignment in which, at first take, his design staff "shrunk back in horror" from this "presumed enemy of creative design." However, in an ideation session, someone drew out a different perspective by inviting people to cite the best "world cars out there" and in doing so discovered that they were all greatly admired designs (the Porsche 911, for example). This rethinking turned the seemingly limited prospect into a juicy design opportunity.

The focus of sales in a high pH firm must be the project design team because only they can make the commitments required to land a project, or in a design competition, develop the design entry. But related logistics and research can effectively be accomplished by a support group of marketing and communication specialists. In any prospect pursuit, the design team needs to understand the client, users, and political, regulatory, physical, and social context of the proposed project. And specialists can gather much of that very effectively. The design team also needs to know the key decision makers and users, if at all possible. While that must be achieved personally by the design team leaders, market specialists can assist in making it happen. The selling of a

[68] Hirshberg, *op. cit.*, p. 63.

high-performance design is highly dependent on developing strong personal relationships with client leaders because it represents a mutual commitment to engage in an arduous quest for enterprise transformation and performance.

There are successful firms that use a continuum between long-term marketing (image building and prospect identification) and sales, where the design team is essentially sold by marketers rather than personally by the team members themselves. That approach does not start a project on a path to achieve a high-performance design.

Markets

The markets function of a practice is to implement public relations strategy; supplement design team efforts in relationship building and prospect identification; develop prospect support tools; support prospect efforts through strategy, research, and presentation assistance; and provide general research and analysis of market needs and trends. In a high pH firm, there is a very close partnership between design teams and market support groups.

The globalization of a practice means significant engagement in foreign markets. In the short term this means finding unique differentiators between a firm's practice and the local practices, and from other foreign competitors who are attractive in that market place. In the longer term, it means addressing whether the practice can satisfy its purpose by being a national firm practicing globally (and therefore remotely) or by becoming a global practice (and thereby practicing locally in multiple countries). The former is often supportable when a firm is following its clients overseas and in the early stages of a developing country when outside expertise is highly valued (overvalued in some cases). As a country's development attitude matures, this model becomes more difficult to sustain, and competition becomes more focused on performance outcomes. In this environment, high pH firms will likely be able to sustain themselves longer than others in practicing globally as a national firm. In the end, though, global practices that have established themselves with a unique and strongly led local presence will be required, and those with high pH will prevail on high-performance design opportunities.

Public Relations and Branding

The purpose of public relations should be to spread the awareness of the firm's values, purpose, and track record (its true brand). This must be done effectively and where it will provide the most benefit to achieving the firm's overall strategy. For a high pH enterprise, this must meet a rigorous test of reality because the expectations and scrutiny of such an entity are high and hyperbole (much less outright bull roar) will not pass muster. The trail a firm leaves doing its projects is the primary reality of its brand for potential clients and for the public. But even for the best firms, word-of-mouth, though important, will not be enough to achieve strategic goals.

Philanthropy

Firm philanthropy is an essential aspect of social responsibility as well as a demonstration of values (your money where your mouth is). The way it is done is as important as what is done. Firm philanthropy has an impact on staff attitudes.

There is always pressure on philanthropy from many directions:

- Not-for-profit clients that seek support
- Clients who seek support for their favored charities
- Staff who have strong views on worthy efforts to support
- Basic human services charities (the social safety net) that simply must get support as part of social obligation
- Arts, environmental, and design centered groups that are heavily dependent on the design professions for their survival

To navigate this sea of near infinite demand in a vessel of finite resource requires the design of approach based on purpose. Such an approach must include priorities that are clearly related to firm purpose and are well articulated as well as mechanisms for decision making, tracking, and reporting. Being in charge of this is not a role for the partner who can't say no in the nicest possible way.

People Development

Because people are the heart of a design enterprise, a high-performance firm must be good at developing people's skills, experience, and leadership as well as developing the kind of firm profile that continues to attract and maintain the best people. Developing people requires a thoughtful approach to mentoring and career development. Talented human resources staff can help define and implement parts of the approach, but for high performance it must be seen as a strategic imperative.

Leadership can be taught. Stimulating creativity can be taught. In both cases, programs tailored to a firm's culture and aspirations are needed to be effective, and these efforts should be rigorous, involving real project work, closely mentored and metrically measured to maximize impact.

Additional skills and knowledge programs are essential to development. While these programs can be more broadly focused, they too should be done with rigor and measured for impact.

Teaching and Learning

Teaching and learning are important to people development. Teaching is important both outside the firm and inside. Outside teaching, particularly but not exclusively at design schools, provides the opportunity to meet students and learn their values and dreams. This has long-term positive effects on the firm in recruiting and in brand perception. Attracting interns and providing valuable experiences for them is particularly valuable because interns are at an inquisitive stage of their development when they are looking for values, and they are close to being a part of the design industry or clients' enterprise.

Teaching inside the firm is essential for staff development at all levels (not just for less experienced staff), and being an organization that values learning is important to creating the environment for continuous growth and development. Teaching and learning within the firm can happen by participation in outside-sponsored programs, and there is value in that type of exposure for infusion and understanding of the mainstream wisdom usually taught in such venues. But for more directed learning focused on the firm's values and purpose, internally designed and implemented programs are most effective. These programs can reinforce values, purpose, and approach and be directed in such a way that they provide continuous challenge and improvement to the firm's basics. They also can convey a sense of personal value to staff.

Leadership Training

A high pH firm is necessarily leadership intensive. Most of us who are leaders in design firms learned those skills on the run by watching and learning from mentors, sometimes supplemented by leadership courses or retreats outside the firm. Because of the need for virtually everyone in a high pH firm to be able to lead at times, traditional learn-by-experience and mentoring need to be supplemented with more focused leadership training. This can only partially be satisfied by programs outside the firm. These won't be specific to the firm's values and culture, so they won't be as effective as internally based, specifically tailored approaches.

Systems

Part of ensuring a firm's high performance is providing the optimum systems for accounting, staff support, and logistics.

Accounting systems must be designed to support project understanding as the prime purpose. They must be open, accessible, and intelligible. Project leaders should have a lot of input to their development both in terms of content and format. Nothing is a bigger waste of design time than hassles over the meaning and accuracy of project accounting. A key part of a high-performance accounting system is relationship building among billing staff, project leadership, and the client's payables staff to ensure smooth communication and early warning on collection anomalies, which are often a leading indicator of client discomfort. These are ways in which the creativity of support staff builds high pH. These systems need to serve the external needs of doing business as well, but those will not improve performance and should not drive the system.

Information systems are the lifeblood of practice, and their performance is critical to achieving high pH. A high-performance information system provides design team support in a way that gives the team broad understanding of possibility and full support for use of capabilities that work for them. In a high-performance environment, design teams will be pushing the envelope on digital system use, and the firm's information system needs to support that while guiding it to affordable means. Information system staff must feel that they are creative partners with design staff and must have great understanding and empathy for the design process. Information systems must first be functional for the design process and second be as convenient for everything else as possible. Integration of systems is a nice ideal but in priority is not as important as the human systems it supports.

Staff support systems (HR), too, must be accessible, legible, accurate, and staff friendly. How these systems are perceived is at least as important as what they cover. Systems that create misunderstandings and hassles negatively impact performance.

Hospitality and logistic systems must be designed to reflect the firm's values and purpose as well. That means that these staff members must feel important to the firm's purpose and have the opportunity to use their own creative potential to help deliver it to clients, visitors, and staff.

Tools

Another part of ensuring a firm's high performance is providing the optimal tools. This is a constantly changing set of needs. A high pH firm will have an easy and understandable way to deal with this, starting with a budgeting process that acknowledges its importance and an understandable non-bureaucratic approval and acquisition process. This system is important in the way it is structured because the desire for tools will always exceed an affordable limit.

But just as important as the tools we select and how we select them is the question, How will we use them?

We are faced with powerful new tools for collaboration and idea generation, which can either improve what we do by our using them to improve processes and effectiveness, or we can fritter them away by focusing on and reinforcing what we do now and by generating complex and meaningless form. Bruce Mau in his work with the Institute Without Boundaries, *Massive Change*, challenged: "Now that we can do anything, what will we do?"

Research

Research is a critical aspect of relevant practice and a difficult function to incorporate. In most firms the bulk of research is done as part of project discovery processes, whether broad inquiry into precedent ideas or focused investigation of material and system alternatives. But this is rarely completely satisfying, and the curious firm will want to do more. Alternatives for this include creating research functions within the firm that try to offset some or even all of their costs by contracted research both around the firm's design work and around outside efforts.

Setting up foundations to provide grant support for outside research that may indirectly apply to the firm's work is another model. The traditional fee-for-service economic model of design firms is not a good one for supporting research in any significant way within the firm's overhead. A change to a value-based business model is both more likely to provide a margin to support research and to demand research to determine value parameters.

The value of research to practice is demonstrated by the impact that digital research has had on Frank Gehry's firm and the KieranTimberlake work on building systems.

Practice at NBBJ

In the 1970s, NBBJ's practice was already 30 years old and was seemingly structured by a combination of default and accounting bias. It had not been consciously designed and was not set up specifically to enhance design performance. Project teams were ad hoc, and the context for them was a rabbit warren spatially and organizationally.

One thing that was positive was that designers mostly stayed with their projects start to finish. However, after the redesign (described below) from a large non-directional partnership to a smaller goal-focused one in the mid 1970s, we seriously began to design the practice to support design.

Strategy

In that early period, strategy development was pretty much an ad hoc event, not rigorously on the agenda. That was when four of us, on a self-selected basis, developed the idea of redesigning the practice and proposed restructuring to a smaller partnership to enable it. A part of that redesign was to align strategy determination (which is a risk setting function) with the major liability for the outcome. That first attempt at firm design dealt with the overall structure and left much to be done relative to all of the other issues that go into designing a successful practice. But it set us on a path of annual analysis of society, the role of architecture and design more broadly, our own motivation, and the possibilities for addressing a practice that could achieve what we wanted. As we got better at this over the years, articulation of values, purpose, and goals emerged along with designs to achieve these.

Strategy became a high priority item on the partners' agenda and was undertaken by the partners, as a group, annually. An important ingredient in our strategy analysis was the diversity in thinking among partners. For instance, Dave Hoedemaker was very focused on people and experience; Friedl Bohm brought a wonderfully broad view of planning, development, and business understanding; and I was both analytical and good at connecting ideas. There were five partners at first, and the number expanded over the years. We found that 10 at the strategy table made the dialogue exponentially less effective, and when it became 12, we reassigned the primary role of strategy development to the board (of five partners) but left ratification to the partnership as a whole.

Initially, our strategy was pretty near term and internally focused to move up the design performance chain. Strategic actions focused on structuring stronger design teams and focusing more on chasing work with higher potential for strong design.

Colleague Firms

As that evolved and we felt a need to broaden the catchment area for that work, we developed a strategy to create a system of collaborations with firms in geographic areas of interest. The strategy was based on our ability to provide building-type expertise and a collaborative approach to be matched with firms that were respected in their markets, shared our design aspirations and willingness to collaborate, and could expand their ability to capture work in their geography by tapping our special expertise.

David Hoedemaker, who was managing partner at the time and the most charming architect you can imagine, led the effort to find these "colleague firms," as we called them, and negotiate verbal agreements to pursue all projects of a pre-agreed nature jointly in their area. We had as many as eight of these arrangements at any time. Most of these resulted in projects. A few were barren and fell away, sometimes replaced by a different colleague in the same area. In some, the collaborations were not well done and caused the relationship to falter. A couple resulted in mergers with us. It was generally a successful approach to expanding our reach and increasing awareness of us as a firm (our brand). It accomplished most of what we set out to do at an affordable cost. It would not be an appropriate strategy for NBBJ in today's reality, where every project team needs to be very carefully crafted for each project opportunity.

At different times we developed strategies to expand our capabilities in areas we thought were essential to providing relevant design.

Project Economics

When project design success or failure was being heavily influenced by the economic analysis of what were then big eight accounting firms, we established our own economics consulting group by capturing a key partner from one of those firms. Our strategy was to integrate the analysis of all aspects of economic performance — impact of facility improvements on operations and revenue, project cost, affordability and bonding capacity — and to do this in plain view rather than the seemingly black box approach of the big eight. We knew that without this open information-sharing approach we would have no credibility, but by opening it to scrutiny by the big eight and by supporting their role in bond evaluation, it was mostly accepted and helped save the design direction of a number of projects. It was particularly effective for us in the health care market, and we expanded it there to become proficient in workload forecasting and operations analysis.

Cost Management

Similarly, in the early 1970s, when construction cost consultants and some bully contractors were causing disruption to design process by inconsistent, ignorant, untimely, panic-inducing, and accusatory approaches to demonstrating the value of their wisdom, we developed a strategy to jump ahead of them with a more accurate and project decision supporting service.

The firm had a reputation for strong cost management based on the work of a very senior partner, Eric Rising (who had worked on the original Yankee Stadium). Eric was very good at anticipating how our designs would develop from concept through construction and had a great reputation and relationship with the best contractors in the Northwest. But he was a loner in his 80s, and times were changing. This was about the time that the wonderful edge-based miracle workers going by the name "value engineering consultants" marched onto the scene and proclaimed to all, You are paying too much, and there is a better way. (They said better, but they meant cheaper). And a lot of bad value decisions were made as a result.

Our strategy was to build a team and a system that would provide parametric-based cost estimates in pre-design and schematic design stages and convert to actual take-off-based estimates at around the design development stage. This would provide a building system by building system tracking of project costs from beginning to end, providing a clear basis for decision making and helping builders understand what they usually missed in their early-stage estimates.

We found an estimator, out of the U.K. quantity surveyor tradition, who was also into computer programming, gave him the staff and IT support he needed, and set up a service called Project Cost Management. Again, our approach was to do this work in an open book fashion to encourage dialogue and credibility. We collaborated with other cost consultants and with builders on our projects, helping them understand how an NBBJ project would likely unfold. We always encourage clients to run parallel cost estimates because of the importance of cost to project success and because of the volatility of markets. This was effective, and it too helped ward off the evil spirits of design sabotage. We gradually melded this service into the design practice to ensure that cost understanding is an integral part of every design team.

We developed similar strategies for other capabilities needed as markets changed: retail design, graphic design, lighting design, and behavioral analysis.

NBBJ has developed strategies for dealing with ownership and leadership transition, globalization, capitalization, new services (and sunsetting services) leadership development, design rigor and content, design approach, and almost anything we could think of that would stimulate or remove obstacles to high design performance.

Financial Strategy

Our capitalization strategy is now very conservative and based on a low level of leveraging. It was not always so, and we learned a couple of hard lessons from that. When I became a partner, we had a CFO who was greatly enamored of the other-people's-money school of finance, and he encouraged maximum profits distribution and operations on a maximized credit line. Within a couple of years of my entering the partnership, there was a credit crunch that sent interest rates soaring and revenues plummeting. Among other hardships, it made the partnership buyouts that were in place untenable. We got through that crisis partly by renegotiating buyouts. But it quite rightly taught us that such a highly leveraged business style has no place for a firm that is focused on its design purpose, not on maximizing financial return.

We later learned another hard lesson from a development venture owned separately by most of the partners, which, though separate, was dependent on the partners' personal wealth. We intended for each project to be based, as most development deals were at the time, on other people's money. But after a handful of modest successes, we took our eye off the ball and let a development manager bet the (our) farm on a big project that took us to the brink. We recovered from that painfully, and each of us had to look at a pretty dumb guy in the mirror for awhile.

What were the lessons learned? There are a number of ways you can endanger a firm's stability. Don't dabble in something that should take your full attention. Don't do it at all if you are building a high pH firm. Don't ever let someone else manage a risky venture for you. And have more respect for your developer clients. If your primary purpose is high-performance design, maintain a relatively high equity base in your firm; do not get caught being over-leveraged at the wrong time (and don't think that you can predict when that will be).

Other important aspects of financial strategy that influence a firm's success include professional-liability and other insurance (know your carrier well; negotiate hard on terms and cost), lease-versus-buy decisions, and managing equity and cash flow. Do not get seduced by high-risk short-term return on money (again, learn from Orange County California and Proctor & Gamble, which both lost big on what their financial advisors assured them were safe high returns).

Development

The development side of practice, in my mind as I became a partner, was externally and relatively near-term focused. I was certainly concerned with sales and marketing and especially concerned with the design reputation side of PR, but brand and all of the internal needs to create a high design performance firm were off my radar screen. It took a long time to come to grips with the interconnectedness of all those things that support the design team and successful creativity. Step by step we pieced that together and came to the realization that firm development is both inclusive of all the external and internal aspects and is a dynamic and continuous need. The sense of what a brand means came hand in hand with understanding that your culture defines who you are, and your accomplishments define what you are.

Sales

To align the focus of project selling with the design teams, we made communication one of the advocacy leaderships of our studios (see the section on team context). Studios generally have four leaders in the core team: design leader, process design leader, technical design leader, and communication design leader (one of whose roles is prospect leadership). Because of the multispecialty nature of the firm, we also have project-type market leaders, who develop many of the personal prospect relationships within the project type, and provide project-type expertise to the project teams in selling and doing projects. These market leaders are part of each studio. The market leaders are very helpful in opportunity screening because of their familiarity with prospects' profiles. Part of their role is to introduce other design team leaders to the potential clients' leaders as early as there is a project prospect, and preferably before the client has decided how it will select a design team. This is the best time to test the climate for high-performance design and to influence the ultimate outcome.

Markets

NBBJ focuses sales within the studio structure and specifically at the project team level. There is a market structure to support each project-type specialty market, headed by a market mentor whose role is to establish strategy, ensure expertise development, set goals, and lead the market leaders in achieving them. These roles cut across studios, are usually filled by partners and principals, and are mostly based in the firm-wide markets studio.

The markets studio takes the production role in producing firm-wide publicity and brochure materials, image management, designing and maintaining the Web site, and providing support to sales and proposal writing. It also provides the organizational structure for market-goal and budget setting and performance tracking. We have tried a number of approaches to market segmentation and integration, which are adjusted frequently relative to market and strategy shifts. Most market definitions have been building-type based but always with some mix of discipline and geography. We have used geography specifically for break-in overseas markets, and sometimes in a three-key matrix, which involves a prospect studio, building-type mentor, and geographic region mentor. At its worst, it is a bureaucratic cat fight. At its best, it has created some of the most powerful project sales efforts.

One of the important issues in marketing for high-performance design is the relationship between a marketing person and the practice as a whole, and the project team specifically. We found that it is difficult to have people who are primarily focused on marketing representing us to potential clients. For that to happen well, those people have to share our design passion and be very good at promoting the design team rather than selling themselves. And they must not make promises they have not vetted with the design team. A common problem in this role is with high achievers who mostly measure success by quantity rather than by appropriateness to firm purpose and brand. That is harmful to the pursuit of high-performance design and wasteful of potential clients' time.

Public Relations

NBBJ went through a period of high focus on design awards and publication in the late 1960s and early '70s initiated by Bill Bain and pushed by David Hoedemaker. In a few years, we went from a minimally published profile to a reasonably respectable one (two *Progressive Architecture* design awards in one year, a national laboratory of the year award, a significant number of local and regional design awards, and numerous publications). This push significantly helped NBBJ's strategic objective to become a multi-regional practice at that time.

Making it happen required spending the time for lead designers to get to know design magazines' staff and editors and learning to present our work effectively.

Late in that push, we tried to define what we thought we were about in an article titled "NBBJ: The Rise of the Regions"[69], where we sought to demonstrate an attitude about design that cut across yet respected regional tradition. That thinking permeated our practice for a number of years.

We also did the typical firm coffee table book in the early 1990s. It became a useful exercise in self-analysis, bringing us face to face with the good, the bad, and the ugly in our body of work. It was helpful in PR and marketing. More than anything, however, it helped us face the gap between our reality and our aspirations and provided an understood level from which we could raise the bar … continuously.

In the early years of the millennium, the third generation of partners — originally led by Rick Buckley and, after his death, by Scott Wyatt, Tim Johnson, and Rich Dallam — took on the task of developing a more focused description of what our practice is about. This is the book described earlier (in NBBJ Purpose), done with the help of Bruce Mau and his fine team. The result was a set of stories about a body of work, which, in various ways, transformed the enterprise for which they were designed. And these stories were largely told in the voice of the clients. The title of the book was *Change Design: Conversations about Architecture as the Ultimate Business Tool.* This was the most effective PR effort the firm had done to that date. It helped define us to ourselves in a very realistic way, and it was perceived by many potential clients as a story that understood their point of view.

Our efforts to publish in the past 10 years or so have achieved a balance among design, business, and trade publications as we have sought to deliver a message about performance.

Philanthropy

Giving has always been a part of the NBBJ ethic going back to the firm's founders. For many years, NBBJ's approach to giving was only generally focused, split between supporting our communities' social safety net, cultural causes in which

[69] *Building Design & Construction*, September 1990, p, 46-52.

we were involved in some way (usually by board participation), and support for not-for-profit clients and other client-sponsored charities. We give both financial support and in-kind support, which we often prefer because it engages the firm in a hands-on way, and of course we give our personal time on boards and committees important to our community citizenship.

As we concentrated more on firm performance, we focused philanthropy more to provide a larger impact in areas that align with our purpose. Most recently, NBBJ is committed to the Nature Conservancy's program to plant a billion trees. The firm is well connected to the Nature Conservancy and has provided important interaction with our staff, reinforcing our values and enriching our staff's experience at the same time.

People Development

NBBJ developed a number of internal people-development programs over time, each with a different purpose and focus. One of the more important things we did was establish an ethic, starting with the partners, that an important part of everyone's responsibility is to find, mentor, and develop someone who could replace you and who is better at what you do than you are. Most of our partners have done this well or are in the process of doing so. It is extremely valuable to the firm's continuing success and something I pride myself on having done well.

As we were beginning to think more about global practice in the 1980s, Pat James, one of our design principals, approached me with an idea that he thought would do a number of things for young staff members and the firm. This program, as mentioned briefly here earlier in NBBJ Curiosity, was called Oregano. The agenda designed for these events exposes participants to culture, politics, art, music, and an inside view of design practices. This brilliant idea develops and rewards young staff, expands the firm's understanding of cross-cultural issues, bonds friendships across studios, and enlivens the design dialogue by fresh perspective from abroad. The program has been continued for nearly 20 years. Among its successes are three young designers who were enlightened by that experience and later became partners in the firm.

NBBJ used a number of outside programs for leadership in the 1960s, '70s, and '80s, but by the time our studio-based culture was demonstrating how leadership-intensive a high-performance design entity was, we realized that we needed something more lasting than even the best few-day seminars, and something that was specifically tailored to our culture.

We had been working for a number of years with David Dunning, an industrial psychologist (first introduced to me by Tony Callison, founder of the firm that today bears his name) who had helped us cope with some of the extremes of creative personalities and had coached a number of people in the firm through difficult times. Rich Dallam took on the task of working with him to define the kind of long-lasting, hands-on program we were seeking.

David worked for nearly a year, drawing on his knowledge of NBBJ, Dallam's insights, and learning from some of the best internal and external leadership programs operating in the United States, to develop a program tailored for us. The result is an annual nine-month program with focused off-site, several-day learning retreats; personal development projects lasting the nine months and involving the individual's current work; and continuous mentoring (typically one-on-two) by respected leader/mentors and periodic evaluation by Dunning and Dallam. We call this program Leading Change. Participation is by the recommendation of studio leadership and sometimes includes the entire leadership team of a project or studio. This program is ongoing, it is judged to be hugely effective, and it mutates periodically based on lessons learned and changing conditions.

Like many firms, we have had a version of internal university for many years, which provides a range of educational topics. The weekly noontime programs currently are called CDIR (from collaboratively developed, intelligently realized) and focus on the craft of buildings, new materials and systems, and the specifics of sustainable strategies. These are fully CE accredited, and credits are automatically tracked with an understood expectation that whether staff are licensed or not, they will gather more credits than licensure requires.

We have run paid summer intern programs in every office and have recruited at select schools to fill those positions. We run those programs to provide a rewarding experience for the interns and the studios that host them. This adds excitement to the practice and is a strong source of high-design talent. We also have participated in the Rice University preceptorships, University of Cincinnati Co-Op program, and the University of Hawaii doctoral candidate practicum program. All of these programs have been mutual learning experiences between our staff and the students and have created valuable long-term relationships. These programs make a significant contribution toward building and maintaining a high pH firm.

Systems

Early on, there were two primary systems that we thought influenced design performance negatively: financial and human resources. The financial system placed a burden on design team leaders through its lack of useful information and seeming disconnect with the design process. The human resource system (benefits primarily) caused staff turmoil through ambiguity and inaccuracy. Later we learned that those issues only scratched the surface of systems problems, and information and communication systems became important as well.

Financial systems were redesigned from the ground up starting from a project perspective (i.e., What can the project team control and what is the most useful and intuitive format in which to provide that?). The basic answer is of course hours and expenses, but what about hourly rates, reimbursable versus non-reimbursable expenses, the impact of actual versus contract allowable overhead, project sales cost, over-long receivables, etc. The design of the reporting and tracking system was done and redone, a trial and error process of ideation and implementation in a partnership between process design leaders and our CFO and her staff. Our CFO, Cece Haw, was a true leader/collaborator in this process, combining genuine admiration and curiosity about design with a creative talent for modifying systems. The result was a system that produced information in terms project leaders asked for, understood, based their process designs on, and used to focus on the things they could control and adjust. Hours, rates, costs for labor, direct expenses (both reimbursable and not), and current billing and collection status were included. It wrapped project leaders into the billing process in a supportive and non-burdensome way and provided them with early warning on a number of indicators. In reality, the design and implementation of the system is always a work in progress because of changing contract conditions and new ideas from process leaders. After project financial systems come studio financial systems, which create combined project and markets performance and add chargeability measures and studio-controlled discretionary costs, and, at times (depending on the dominant mood of studio process leaders), has included variations in the overhead allocation model. The latter includes such concepts as studio space quantity as a studio controllable, which at times of very aggressive gaming-focused process leaders is something they crave to deal with until they learn that focusing on such minutiae is much less effective than focusing on design projects, at which time it cycles back.

The determination of the studio financial model is a continuous negotiation among studio process leaders supported by accounting. We have allowed that continuous dialogue because it has given staff control of their destiny, has produced very creative approaches, is a great learning process for design and accounting staff, and has virtually eliminated the old "they" that causes so much havoc. Some of the benefits of this constant creative abrasion approach are that it creates passion around protecting the design process from financial tyranny, and process leaders have become great educators of all studio staff about how project and studio economics work. This provides another process to develop future leaders.

Finally, the firm-wide reporting system was also rebuilt from the ground up, this time from the perspective of what the principals and partners are interested in and what format they can readily grasp. Although none of the financial or accounting information essential to running a business can be sacrificed in developing these reporting systems, they are not in an accounting language with which most accountants are immediately familiar. Rather, they are in language that is specifically designed both to enable strong financial performance and reduce friction for the design process. Generally for us, this means multipliers, collections, net and gross profits, market performance (cost/capture), backlog in a few meaningful formats (under contract and underway, contracted but on hold or not started, and selected not contracted). Of course, we track banking ratios as well, but being well capitalized, these are not front-of-mind.

The accounting side of our administrative studio also provides key support for the billing/collecting aspect of projects. This is a partnership with project process leaders in setting up each project's billing system protocol, establishing a relationship with the client's payables staff, ensuring bill-to-pay compatibility, and closely monitoring the collection cycle to provide early warning advice and jointly strategizing remedy when needed. They also maintain historic data on project performance with project characteristics for aid in future fee proposals. All of this is part of the support design purpose mantra of the administrative studio.

The compensation strategy of the firm has been to keep salaries at or slightly above the industry means and supplement that with well defined, reliable, and reasonably generous performance bonuses. In this case, well defined means based on preset performance criteria, which ties to firm financial transparency. On top of that, there are more subjectively distributed bonuses (but from a well defined bonus pool) for titled staff. We have tried to maintain as much stability in this system as possible to maintain staff confidence in it and have been transparent in showing how firm profits are used. The issue for design performance is that, generally, money is not a primary motivator for creativity, but any sense of inequity is a great de-motivator for it.

The HR side of the admin studio is focused on making benefits understandable, with easily accessible and accurately maintained status indicators. Our strategy on benefits is to provide a narrow and understandable range of choices to allow for the differences in staff needs, and to keep the overall benefit package in the mid- to slightly above-average range for the industry, again to keep the focus on design rather than perceived economic injustice.

Tools

We have tried to be rigorous in setting priorities for tool acquisition and maintenance and have set affordable budget limits to work within, based on benchmarking against other enterprises combined with judgment based on strategic priorities. To set priorities within the available resources, we create a group of users from the studios, visionaries, and IT staff to generate an initial wish list. That list is prioritized by studio leaders who also make the ROI case for their priorities. A final direction is set by the firm core team of managing partners who sometimes interject a new strategic priority. There is a shared responsibility at every stage in this to ensure that we find and incorporate transformational directions and that we maintain a lean attitude.

Maintenance and upgrades of the primary communication and design tool sets always consume the majority of the available resources, but the more discretionary minority budget has its priorities change somewhat with strategic imperatives. For example, after seeing the effectiveness of physical models and prototyping both in our own Los Angeles studio and in our brief collaboration with Renzo Piano, we pushed to create a much stronger and more accessible model building capability, adding tools (3-D printers, laser cutters, etc.), along with space and experts to do that. Similarly, parametric modeling/generative components received a focused push, and interactive smart screens received a push as part of integrated project delivery.

Research

Among the many philanthropic legacies that founding partner Floyd Naramore left behind was an architectural research foundation administered by NBBJ partners, which initially gave modest grants for architectural research. I applied for and was granted one in my earliest years at NBBJ. I researched health care concepts in Europe, specifically a concept called the area industrial zone, a somewhat revolutionary idea at the time. Through that effort I was exposed to interesting projects and ideas, which influenced my thinking and our design approach, gave me material for speaking and publishing, and created some valuable relationships. This was not only a personally rewarding and skill developing event, it was very beneficial to the firm. The investment was modest — a couple of months of my time — and the research grant covered expenses. It convinced me that modest investment in research can provide high return. Unfortunately for us, the tax rules governing the foundation changed to make firm staff ineligible.

We have encouraged personal initiative in research in many small ways by funding small investments of time for self-initiated and focused efforts. These have related to a range of topics, such as materials, sustainability, and digital systems. Just as often, however, we have resisted grander proposals that did not have clear, achievable objectives. We have encouraged project-based research, and quite a bit has been done that way. We view our Oregano program as a research endeavor, and it has provided that benefit. We have been approached to partner with academic faculty on projects, but so far have not found the opportunity that matched our strategic priorities and affordability criteria with faculty objectives and needs.

We have also tried to maximize the research benefit from project-specific investigation, which includes a broad range of topics from social issues to physical systems and materials. We developed a new building typology for health care (which separated temporal and permanent building aspects, creating a growth system with a built-in attitude about people and daylight — which I dubbed "autogenesic" and seems to puzzle rather than enlighten many — through building it step by step through three design competitions and implementing much of it in a couple of later projects.

We supported a partially co-funded development of a new approach to operating rooms (OR21), which has led to a lot of worthwhile relationships for us.

Practice at Danish Firms

All of these firms are partnerships, ranging from recently formed first-generation firms, to mature first-generation, to second- and third-generation. Their practices reflect their level of maturity in the issues that they address. Their sales are largely design-competition focused, a part of the reality of life in the European Union. Most of these design competitions are either selectively invited or at least prequalified.

3XN is a mature first-generation firm, now with five partners, headed by founding partner Kim Herforth Nielsen. They have a six-person board (three outside members plus three partners), which adds to the partners' perspective, but the firm's strategy is mostly intuitive and initiated by Nielsen. He is aware of a need to reinvent the firm periodically (on the "madonna curve" as he describes it). He views the blogosphere as a powerful tool shaping what's next. The firm is establishing itself with a global signature in educational and cultural projects. Their GXN entity adds a leading technical edge caché to the brand.

Much of their sales are design competition-based. Their marketing and public relations include a sophisticated Web site with extensive video clips, and they recently mounted a major exhibition, "Mind Your Behaviour," at the Danish Architectural Center.

Arkitema is an early second-generation firm (with most of the first generation still active in the practice, though, as already mentioned, retiring as a group in 2010). They have a four-person board (two outside members and two firm partners) who influence strategy.

They executed a strategic merger in 2004 and are in a staged transition on another potential merger.

They have branded themselves as aggressive in construction technology and user interface.

The majority of their sales are design competition-driven. They have used their focus on construction optimization to create the related construction product development group Arkitema Prefab. They have a fixture, product, furniture design entity called Arkitema Design, and they brand their specialty practices by name: Arkitema Living, Arkitema Workspace, Akitema Learning, Arkitema Health, etc.

The firm develops people through training but also by integrating learning into all phases of their work through team evaluation and discussion. They run a staff development/education program called The Arkidemy, which ties to annual staff development interviews and includes five skill development areas:

- Creative and innovative
- Learning
- Social
- Communication
- Self-management

They seem to be the most systems-conscious of these firms. They introduced a structure of job and people managers, "precept" (pre-design) and project managers and creative managers in 2007. Much of the firm's development seems to have come from a research focus.

BIG is the youngest first-generation practice, founded by Bjarke Ingels, who now has five partners and two associate partners. Their strategy is to be the firm that shakes things up by being radically accommodating through making opportunity out of conflict, restating the issues, and embracing opposing viewpoints to discover the solutions that solve for all of them. A prime example is their unrealized project for housing on a football and garden patch venue that won support from all constituents by giving each something they valued.

BIG gets most of its work from competitions but also generates work by looking for unannounced needs. The Danish Maritime Museum at Helsingor is an interesting hybrid in which the competition win was challenged (for a solution outside a dogmatic interpretation of the rules box). So the client cancelled the competition and hired the firm anyway. The leaders promote the firm and its ideas by a constant stream of creative releases like the "archicomic" and recently by Ingels' lecture on TED and his participation in the film on free running My Playground by Kasper Astrup Schroder.

So far, the firm's people development seems focused on diversity in hiring.

The primary heuristic of the firm is the attitude of creative accommodation encapsulated in "Yes is more."

C.F.Moller is a third-generation practice, with a strong legacy from its founder, who was both a teacher and an architect. Their strategy is developed by the nine partners and is currently aimed at practicing globally based on their strongly Nordic approach. The firm has office presence in three locations in Denmark, plus Oslo, Stockholm, and London. The firm's brand is tied to its Scandinavian ethic of simplicity, clarity, and unpretentiousness, which is highly effective in many markets. It has projects in Africa, Asia, and India and has tried work in southern Europe, where the partners felt priced out of the market. Most of the work (about 85 percent) is gained by competition. It is the most mature practice in development of internal systems.

Henning Larsen is a second-generation firm, also with a strong legacy from its namesake founder, who developed an international practice early. There are six partners who develop strategy together. A majority of the work comes from competitions. In addition to its Scandinavian presence, the firm is active in the Middle East and China. Its international strategy is to seek work where the partners think there is an opportunity to make positive change. One of the heuristics the firm employs is a "visual matrix multi-criteria based assessment decision assist tool" (focused on sustainability). The partners have embraced sustainability research by supporting three doctoral students from the technical university to bring sustainable strategies to the firm's work. The partners administer a foundation set up by Henning Larsen that has supported research by some of the leaders of other Danish firms (although it does not directly benefit the firm).

Schmidt Hammer Lassen is a mature first-generation firm with much of the second generation leadership in place and a total of five partners and three associate partners. Strategy has been developed in a broadly inclusive way with many staff participating. The firm went through an ambitious process of defining its future, which in some way engaged nearly everyone in the firm. The effort lasted two years and produced three manifestos describing what the firm is and where it is headed, a remarkable joint effort of the partners with other leaders in the firm. This visioning process was also a very strong staff development exercise, exposing everyone to a broad spectrum of practice issues.

The firm has succeeded in achieving a high percentage of repeat work, which has reduced its reliance on design competitions to less than a majority. It supports doctoral research in environmental dimensions of urban residential projects and in fabric-formed concrete. It uses BIM in environmental analysis and simulation.

Offices are in Aarhus, Copenhagen, Oslo, London, and Shanghai. Projects are in Sweden, Germany, the United Kingdom, the Netherlands, and China. The firm designs products, primarily from defined project needs, and has a number of them currently offered by Danish companies.

BUSINESS MODEL

A design enterprise business model must be consistent with practice values and purpose if it is to support high performance. If the business model is not based on and carried out with the same ideals professed in its purpose and values, it will undermine the focus of the staff and the trust of clients.

A design enterprise can be designed primarily as a high earnings and profit engine through providing basic service at an attractive price, where the transactions and service rather than the projects are the firm's *raison d'être*. There are many clients who value that; therefore, there is a large market for it. As you will be aware by now, this book is not aimed at that type of practice and has little to offer it.

Another business-focused model that has shown great strength in the marketplace in recent years is based on building maximum market share through practice compiling that creates broad geographic and discipline coverage. There is a strong financial incentive for that because in taking such an entity public (which requires a very large revenue base and growth record) a capitalization rate can be achieved that values the firm well beyond what an internal ownership transition could produce. However, that too is a poor model for creating a high pH firm for reasons that I trust are apparent, the most important two being the divorce between leadership and ownership and the basic purpose of the firm. So there is nothing here for that type of practice either.

Because of the need for a passionately held sense of purpose and a personally lived set of values, a high pH firm must be owned and controlled by its leaders; this means closely held. A partnership is a robust model for this, but closely held corporate structure can work as well, as long as stock exchange rules keep it in the hands of active practitioners.

During the past hundred years or so, architectural design firms have practiced primarily on a fee-for-service business model. That model prices its service based predominately on a ratio to the construction cost of the projects and, to a lesser extent, based on a multiple of time-card cost. Either approach is always, of course, subject to negotiation in the context of market conditions. In this business model, the primary factors tracked to determine economic performance on an individual project basis are project multiplier, chargeability, and prospect or marketing cost, and the enterprise-wide basis adds non-project-based overhead costs. The model is relatively simple to understand and track, and it seems like a relic.

Fee-for-service, in part at least, was intended to ensure the objectivity of the designer in representing the client's interest while also objectively interpreting the building contract documents. With the liability insured and risk-averse attitude of the profession, it has not delivered well on that objective. And, very important, compensation bears no relationship to value delivered.

While this continues to be a dominant business model, a more value-based model is appropriate for high-performance design. This is a model in which the long-term value that the project delivers through a transformation of client enterprise is recognized, and the risk of delivering that value is shared.

The recent adoption of various integrated project delivery-based agreements—where owner, builder, and designer share risk and reward on a formulaic approach based on project delivery goals — is a step in that direction. But I am talking about inclusion of performance goals beyond the project delivery realm and into the realm of project performance for the purpose intended. It can include aspects of revenue or market share or creativity, whatever the client has agreed is the transformation that is important. The compensation for success should be factored from this value, and the designer should share some risk for disappointing performance. This approach requires development of good metrics and a strong partnership between owner and designer, and preferably builder. This business model focuses a practice on high performance.

Business Model at NBBJ

NBBJ is a fee-for-service based partnership model. As indicated earlier we have had successful experience with designer lead design- build and more recently have undertaken a handful of integrated project delivery contracts, which begins to stretch the meaning of that, and have explored a more value-delivered approach with a few clients. We have not made the leap into a true value-based model. That is on the long-term strategic agenda, but we will have to find a (so far) unique opportunity to start that transformation.

The partnership model has the symbolic strength and the structural flexibility to meet all of our needs at our current size (750+/-), but we periodically look at alternatives and feel that other structures may work. Note that the partnership is the primary way the firm operates, but we have other structures where required by local jurisdiction, just as any multi-jurisdiction entity must.

To us, the psychology of having partners is different than having fellow officers or directors, maybe in a way that is analogous to family versus business associates. There is more of an implied commitment to common purpose and a very real shared professional and financial position. There is no corporate "they," there is only "we."

Business Models in Danish Firms

All six of these Danish Firms operate on a fee-for-service model. All are partnerships, most a limited liability form.

Several engage in product design in some form (which they say is self-sustaining but not a cash cow) and all engage in significant consultancy work on lump-sum or time-and-expense basis.

STRUCTURE

Team/context/support, leadership and ownership, place

Structure is essential to effectiveness. You may view it as the toll that must be paid to minimize frustration and wasted time finding the stuff needed to do the work and keep track of product, people, facility, and finances. But structure's purpose is to support the work of design and make a viable, legal, and financially sound professional and business entity, not to dominate it. The firm's structure can make a positive contribution to a high design performance environment if it is designed, purposed, recognized, and rewarded to do that.

How the structure is presented is important in how it is perceived by both design and support staff. The presentation must match the reality, but it also influences the reality. You can say that support staff are critical to design success, but if you don't mean it, they will still be critical to it while being critical of it. And it is important to present the structure so that people can see themselves as part of the design purpose. For the structure to be most effective, it should be clear, focused, and as simple as possible and demonstrate that design is the primary purpose.

Team/Context/Support

The *raison d'être* of a design firm is in the projects it completes. The most important element of the practice is the project-focused team. Project teams, however, exist in a habitat beyond the context of a single project, and how they are engaged and supported outside the project experience is critical to their long-term development and to the enterprise's long-term success. A studio model is one example of a habitat for project teams. Every project team needs support for tasks that are essential to the project and the business but are not directly a part of the design and implementation process (from billings to printing and employee benefits).These support functions can be departmentalized, but they may be better aligned with design purpose if placed in a studio model of their own. Being in a studio model, particularly if given the same strong sense of purpose as a design studio, seems to energize creativity in support of design.

Project Teams

Who should be considered a part of a project design team? Everyone necessary to accomplish the work. That seems simple enough, but how often is everyone thought of and included in initial project discovery and ideation? Not often, in many practices. Why do you want input (or buy-in) from a cost expert, a materials expert, or a codes expert at an early stage? Think about that. You are in the most formative stage of something, the ultimate success of which will be heavily influenced by all three. You want any ideas possible from these perspectives that might trigger a breakthrough strategy, and you want these individuals to understand project goals and concepts thoroughly. So how do you incorporate all of the players at a time when you want to rock 'n' roll and get a concept going? Project process and leadership are the keys to making this work. With intelligent and creative leadership and a rigorous process, you can get just the right interaction without making the whole process inefficient. Project leadership must cover the major skill bases, act collaboratively, and foster collaboration in others. Every project is unique, so an appropriate leadership must be tailored for that. The leadership team on an architectural project might include the lead process designer, lead technical designer, lead architectural designer, lead interior designer, and lead landscape designer. But others who might be important are lead building type specialist, a lead behaviorist, or a lead urban planner. Note that these are project roles, not firm titles. Partners or principals could presumably fill any of these roles.

With strong collaborative leadership in place, a process can be designed for the project that is both inclusive and efficient.

However the project team is structured, it will be its most creative if the ultimate responsibility and authority for the outcome resides within the team, and the team has ample opportunity to enlist outside critique and ideas as it sees fit. And it will be most creative if it lives in an environment that maximizes positive creative stimulation and minimizes obstacles to creativity.

Amabile[70] identifies nine environmental stimulants, eight of which I believe should be internal to the team (under their control) and one of which is external. Paraphrasing, the internal stimulants include freedom of choice in what and how to do something, good project management (I would say leadership instead), sufficient resources, encouragement and enthusiasm for new ideas,

70 Amabile, *op. cit.* p. 231-232.

recognition, sufficient time for creative exploration, challenging projects, and a sense of urgency. The external stimulant is an organizational mechanism or culture (for considering new ideas, providing a climate of cooperation and collaboration across organizational entities, prizing innovation, and ensuring that failure is not catastrophic).

The environmental obstacles also include nine, but of these I think only four should be considered internal to the design team and the other five are organizational responsibility. Again paraphrasing, the internal obstacles include constraint on work methodology, poor project management (again I prefer leadership), inappropriate feedback and critique, and reluctance to change or take risk. The external (organizational) obstacles are corporate characteristics (of inappropriate reward, bureaucracy, non-collaboration, and low value on innovation), organizational disinterest in project, insufficient resources, inappropriate time pressure, and internal (intra-organizational) competition. This set of stimulants and obstacles is useful to understand in setting guardrails for high design performance teams.

An important item on both the stimulants and obstacles list is time. This is important to designing a practice for performance: Time pressure is real and the design process must be effective to cope with the pressure without it becoming destructive to creativity. That is why process design and creative stimulation are both so important.

A theoretically ideal team from the perspective of any single project's design integrity and consistency is one that starts a project at the pre-ideation stage (discovery, definition) and follows it (intact) through to completion of construction and occupancy. Why is this so? It ensures that everyone influencing the outcome of the project shares a deep understanding of the purpose and success measures of the project, understands and owns the design resolution, is capable and committed to apply that consistently down to the last detail in documentation, and works to preserve it through the final reality and use of the project. It eliminates information degradation caused by hand-offs.

But is this ideal the best approach in the real world? No. In the reality of project life, it is not efficient to have all of the staff on the project continuously, and it is probably impossible to develop a process design that works and accomplishes that kind of complete team continuity. The opposite, however—a team that is totally discontinuous, based solely on the demands of efficient use of time in a total practice environment—is disastrous to the purpose of design. The real ideal lies in a team that approximates the design integrity model (total staff engaged and knowledgeable) while optimizing effectiveness (needed staff there at the beginning and thereafter always available at the moment of need).

Ad Hoc Teams

Project teams might be completely ad hoc, drawn together based solely on experience and talent credentials tailored to a specific project. This has the clear advantages of an all-star team in sports. But it also has the disadvantages of an all-star team: unfamiliarity with other team members, no long-term opportunity to optimize for team strengths, no cohesive vision, and likely differing perceptions of goals.

The practical reality of this approach is that it encourages short-term commitment to a project and often premature exit and inadequate focus from key players.

Permanent Teams

Project teams that stay together project after project, however, have the advantage of developing optimum ways of working together and share both a common vision and perception of goals and priorities.

The disadvantage to this approach is that it limits the kind of spark that can come from including a new perspective in the mix or a specific experience base that could accelerate the team's learning curve about the demands of specific building typologies. Further, the practical realities are that so few projects continue unabated from start to finish that such teams are often caught in an awkward juggle of two or more projects trying to maintain reasonable chargeability.

Context Makes a Difference

Placing teams in the context of a small studio that has staff for two to four simultaneous projects can provide many of the advantages of both approaches and can also ameliorate some of the disadvantages of each. In this environment, all of the studio members know each other well, they all understand their values and goals, and they can be quite knowledgeable about all projects in the studio.

Context and Studio Habitat

Project teams are the building blocks for practice success. But it is how these teams behave that is critical. And critical to how they behave is how they are formed and the support of the environment in which they live. Models of structure for this include:

Ad hoc project teams drawn from all staff resources (discussed above)

Permanent teams staying together across multiple projects (also discussed above)

- Studio-based teams
    - Designer-led studios
    - Partner-led studios
    - Market-, geography- or building type-based studios (led by a market leader)
    - Core team-led studios (collaborative leadership)
- Competition teams/implementation teams (in a design competition focused environment)
- Design teams/implementation teams (similar to above but in a non-design competition focused environment).

The choice of any of these (or other) approaches should be based on the belief that the approach is the best way to achieve the practice's purpose. This is influenced by the markets in which the firm practices and by the personality of its leadership. The danger is that an approach will be selected that suits the comfort zone of the firm's leadership without real design optimization for purpose. You will know that has happened when the primary justification for the approach is "That is the way I work best." My bias is clearly for a collaboratively led studio model that does not separate design from implementation.

A small studio-based environment is an effective model for high-performance design in any enterprise larger than about 80 total staff. We have let individual studios grow to a size as large as 85, and by that time they had become unwieldy. Tom Kelley says that IDEO's studio system was started in the mid-1990s as they approached the 100-person size.[71] Lars Due of Arkitema said their firm found 18 to 20 worked for them.

---

[71] Kelley, *op. cit.*, p. 72.

A studio environment, as I am defining it is a semi-autonomous practice within the larger context of a design enterprise.

A studio within a larger practice has the advantage that its size can be managed to maintain close personal and mentoring relationships, a sense of belonging, and (importantly if enabled well) a sense of self-direction and responsibility.

One caution about a multi-studio organization, however, is that it can create internally focused competition, which can have both negative and positive impacts on creativity. Amabile states: "Win-lose competition between peers has a negative effect on creativity ... competition with outside groups may have a positive effect on the creativity of work teams."[72]

In my experience, competition on project outcome quality between project teams (and between studios) is generally positive because other projects are seen as external by a team, and that kind of competition is energizing. But competition over economic performance can be quite the opposite. It is more typically seen as an internal competition over extrinsic reward and can be negative under normal circumstances. In structuring a studio system, it must be carefully designed to align incentives knowledgeably relative to the desired outcome of design performance.

Designing, testing, and refining human systems is key to organizational transformation and is a hallmark of high pH firms. It is a cultural attribute that only comes from acknowledging the potential benefit, doing it a first time, seeing benefit, refining, trying again, and continuing. It will not happen if there is not a genuine commitment to change. In any organization there is a huge inertia working against change. That inertia is built of comfort with personal status quo, fear of unknown, and fear of failure. Initiating and sustaining a culture willing to refine and redefine its human systems continuously requires leadership as change agent. Since we as designers are change agents for our clients and users (wittingly or not) it seems particularly important that we embrace change ourselves and learn how to implement it with and for others.

Support

The way that design teams and studios are supported by enterprise functions — such as accounting and finance, human resources, facilities, supply and logistic services, reception and administration, any of these things — influ-

[72] Amabile, *op. cit.*, p. 240.

ences the success or failure of a high-performance creative habitat. Each of these functions can either be a demonstration of the culture's value of design or can belie it by attitudes and actions. If everyone in these support functions believes that high-performance design results are their ultimate aim, they will take it seriously when designing their procedures and methods. To be avoided is designing to the most familiar or easiest approach or by management-centered norms they may have picked up in business school or from prior corporate experience.

To get to a design outcome-focused support group, you have to find leaders who come to the design enterprise because they are fascinated and energized by its creative nature. Often these people will begin their biographical discussion by saying: "I always wanted to be a designer." You have to help them understand the design process. A good approach for that is to let them participate in a design project. And you should encourage their participation in open design critiques and remind them that a good idea doesn't care where it came from. Jerry Hirshberg tells the story of an executive secretary, Cathy Wu, who broke an impasse in the design of the Cocoon concept vehicle by having the courage at a mid-stage critique to say that the proposal at that stage, "just looks fat, dumb, and ugly to me!" This broke through the refinement dialogue that the team was trapped in and encouraged them to seek a much stronger basic solution.[73]

When a support group is given a clear sense of purpose to enable high design performance, it can unleash creativity to invent new ways of doing that are anything but bureaucratic.

---

73 Hirshberg, *op. cit.*, p. 58.

Structure at NBBJ

NBBJ in the 1960s was a firm of about 60 people organized around ad hoc project teams assembled for each project. At that time there was a significant change happening in the marketplace, from a majority of work coming to firms on a direct select basis (based on personal relationships and referrals) to a qualifications based interview selection process. In that environment, project teams were put together as much for their sales skills (which were pitiful) as for their real commitment to the project. We quickly became good at this approach and retained a former market leader from the Boeing Co., Henry Ash, to school us on sales presentations. Henry was the son of an Austrian theater impresario. His favorite critique was: "How much less could you say?" That was double entendre for both *You talked a lot and said nothing* and *Truly, try to distill your message to fewer words.* For a period of time a few of us had a remarkable record of winning projects through this approach and Henry's coaching. However, we soon realized that winning the work with a team that looked and sounded good but was neither fully committed nor really the most skilled for the assignment did not produce satisfyingly good projects.

The practice was administered by a former big eight accountant, Harry Widener, who managed a layered system of support functions: reception, secretarial, administrative, print room, accounting, and the early embryo of IT (at that time primarily an accounting tool). After his untimely death, we tried several practice manager/CEO models with non-architects and with very management-oriented architects. As soon as we began taking our culture seriously, though, we felt that running the firm, both in reality and symbolically, had to be in the hands of a design-oriented partner to keep the firm focused on what we were about — design. And at that time we placed firm leadership clearly in the hands of a design-focused architect, David Hoedemaker.

As we began conscious design of the practice, we periodically attempted to diagram our structure. I have a laughable notebook of organization charts that look like early electronic circuit boards, and I remember great pain in trying to explain to staff what they meant and why they were a good thing. Without a sense of humor I would have died a thousand deaths (whereas two or three were plenty).

In 1983, when our staff size was about 280, we relocated our Seattle office to renovated warehouse space and I undertook the CEO role for the western two-thirds of NBBJ. We used this as an opportunity to reinvent and transform our practice approach. Part of that was to go to an all open-space work environment, which changed the way project teams were able to work together.

An even bigger change was to initiate a studio approach.

We had a design team led by a couple of principals who had previously worked at Caudill Rowlett Scott — Dennis Forsyth and Pat James. They were motivated to create a collaboratively led practice studio. Fortunately, we had a large project as an anchor for that start-up and gave it a try. We created a studio based on a small group of people practicing as a semi-autonomous group within the firm, taking responsibility for their own projects and for implementing the firm's values, purpose, goals, and strategy as related to their realm of the practice. This was first initiated as a single studio experiment. As that studio demonstrated the success of a group that could focus on its own set of projects, control its own resources, and create its own subculture, it was recognized as a big improvement in the pursuit of excellence. The self-selection and motivation of that studio group soon became the envy of most of the firm, and a majority of staff clamored to practice the same way. This made implementation of a firm-wide studio system relatively painless.

Within three years the entire firm was on a studio basis, including support functions whose members found the studio model an energizing recognition of their role and importance to the design process.

That initial studio led by a few transformation-focused leaders also pioneered an approach to project involvement mandating that every staff member assigned to a project was on that project from start to finish. Making this work meant creating job processes that rebalanced the traditional staff-loading bell curve, typically delving into technical solutions much earlier and testing just-in-time delivery of some systems at the end. The benefit of this approach is an elimination of most of the error-inducing knowledge transfer inherent in the more traditional and sequential team involvement approach.

This too was a powerful experiment for us and forever changed the firm mentality about staffing and workflow. Of course, as I have said, in the real world the absolute ideal of start-to-finish even workflow is rare except on the smallest and most time-constrained projects. But this thinking leads to developing project processes that minimize handoffs and unnecessary duplication of effort, similar to many aspects of the Toyota Product Development approach (not the Toyota Production System).

With multiple design studios in operation, we were able to develop our project design team ideas from what was working in various studio environments. We sought strong project leaders who would take joint responsibility for project outcome and teach their teams to think that way as well. We evolved to a project core team structure of four to six people, including architectural design leader, process design leader, communications design leader (often the clients' primary focus), technical design leader, and interiors or building type leader. You will notice that every role title includes design, emphasizing that everyone must be a designer.

NBBJ started with a notion that about 30 people was a good size for a studio, in a practice that had a range of projects from 25,000 square feet to 3 million square feet. At that size, everyone can be reasonably aware of all projects in the studio, mentoring can be very intimate, and communication and participation are immediate. Over 25 years or so, we let studios grow to as large as 85 people and tried to establish a studio culture with as few as 10 (these smaller studios were usually focused in a discipline such as graphics or lighting). The large end of these extremes was never successful or sustainable for long. The small end is a struggle, but for some specialty groups it is workable.

We evolved the studios as performance centers with performance goals that they negotiated with each other and with firm-wide leadership.

On the design side, we used surrogate performance measures, such as design awards and work published, as well as design leaders' evaluation and internal project evaluation.

On the financial side, we experimented with a wide range of firm overhead allocation methodologies. The initial methodology was set up by our CFO and me, aimed at having studios responsible only for what they could directly control and with as few things to track as reasonable (initially multiplier, chargeability, market cost, and backlog ratios).Receivables were added not long after. Over the years, as studio leaders became better at dealing with their studios' performance, there was a cycle of negotiating different kinds of controllables for which they wanted responsibility, sometimes more, occasionally fewer as they tested the effects on their focus for design. Ultimately, though, we were seeking financial performance that could support all of our goals for design performance, development, financial stability, equitable staff compensation, and reasonable return for partners .For this we felt that a profit of 20 percent of net fee revenue was reasonable at the studio level.

We often have used single studios as a test bed for a new idea, setting specific criteria for success. These opportunities are eagerly sought for the most part and many are self-initiated.

An unanticipated but powerful benefit of multiple studios in a single location was the stimulus they gave each other in design, practice methods, technology and cultural milieu. It became NBBJ's goal to have more than one studio in every location, a goal that takes time to fulfill and one of the few appropriate reasons to seek growth. A substitute for this is great connectivity across locations, which we also seek.

That reorganization snowballed: In addition to the studio change, we started a sweeping change in human systems. We organized our support functions into studios as well. We did this to provide a supportive context for these functions and encourage the development of studio culture around a sense of purpose (to enable high design performance). Administration is a studio, and markets is a studio. Both are virtual studios since they serve and have staff in multiple locations. Both studios have created a sense of camaraderie, and both have been creative in defining and implementing service that is supportive of design. When I joined NBBJ in the heyday of sexism, the only comment I heard about our reception function was how attractive the ladies were. In recent years, I have heard from many clients, vendors, and contractors about how helpful and focused our receptionists are, whether they encounter them in person or on the telephone. Our accounting and human resource staffs have found ways to partner with design project staff, whether in effective and personable billing and collections or readily accessed and accurate benefits information delivered in a way that appears to advocate for the individual.

Other firm-wide support groups we fostered include design leaders, process leaders, delivery leaders, and several project-type groups such as health care and research. These groups create their own agendas. They meet face-to-face a few times a year and virtually on a more regular basis. Several of them regularly invited outside critics, designers, and industry leaders to give feedback about our work. They pushed for and usually got directness in those encounters, so they were both interesting and applicable to our work.

By the mid 1990s, we finally were able to boil down our structural diagram to a simple inverted pyramid, with clients and their projects in the wide band at the top, project teams and their studios directly below that, support and market studios below that, the firm core team below that, and the partners and board at the tiny bottom end (well grounded, as I like to view it). See figure 3. That seems to encapsulate a lot of attitude and approach in a very simple way.

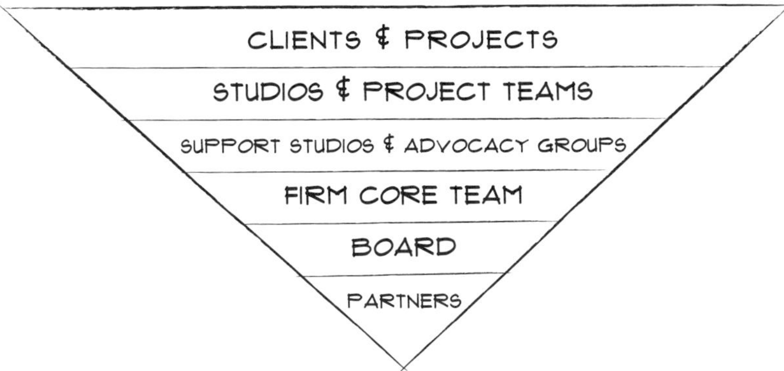

Figure 3. *NBBJ structure chart, c. 1995*

Structure at Danish Firms

Though some of this information overlaps with material covered in prior context, it is included again here for clarity.

3XN, with staff of 100 and five partners, is structured as one studio, though in two locations (Aarhus and Copenhagen), each of which has a competition department. The partners describe their structure as a project-oriented network, with continuous interchange of staff and ideas between offices. They assign a primary and a secondary (backup) partner to head every project team. The rest of the project team structure is a head of project, project manager, design manager, and maybe a planning manager and project architect. The competition departments are headed by partners. A partner is CEO. Administrative staff includes a non-partner CFO, a head of international markets, and a public relations manager.

Arkitema has 13 partners (until the retirements previously mentioned) with a staff of about 160, though as recently as 2005, the firm has been as large as 260. Each of their four offices is called a studio, though Stockholm and Beijing are both very small and supported by offices in Denmark. There is a non-partner, non-architect managing director (soon to be made a partner).

Project teams are non-hierarchical and composed to "ensure that the skills of individual staff members are both fully utilized and challenged."

The firm's project process, called "Arkitema sensemaking," is described as a "carefully prepared and organized . . . . User-integrated design process."

Projects are headed by creative managers who represent Arkitema to the clients from inception onward. The firm identifies 19 people filling that role, including seven of the partners. Its support structure is headed by managers for administration, human resources, job management, communication, and agreements and technology (including IT).

BIG has about 95 people and currently has six partners and two associate partners, one who is a non-architect managing director and another who is an architect business developer.

The project team approach is ad hoc but within the scale of an open environment for 95 people. The process pretty much engages the whole team from start to finish, and because of the innovation in form and determination to make it practical, the team is influenced by technical designers being on the team early in the process.

C.F. Moller is currently about 320 people in seven locations, with nine partners. The partners run the company, with Tom Danielsen currently the managing partner and Lars Kirkegaard accounting partner. The firm has competition design teams. Project teams are formed ad hoc in alignment with building-type experience, health care being one of the dominant ones.

Henning Lassen has about 130 people and six partners, (limited liability form) and has a management team of three partners, Mette Kynne Frandsen as CEO, and an international design director and design director for Scandinavia. The firm is divided loosely into two groups by this geography of markets, with building specialization cutting across them. It uses competition teams with the follow-on team drawn from the geographic groups supplemented by building specialists.

The firm also has small project-related offices in Riyadh, Reykjavik, and Damascus.

Schmidt Hammer Lassen has just over 140 staff and five partners. The firm has a non-partner accountant CEO. It went through a structural redesign at about year 12 of the practice. That redesign created a series of departments, including human resources, proposal writing, and accounting. There is a board of directors with three outside members and two partners. The board has provided a lot of sound advice and added perspective on direction. The project team approach here is also one of design competition teams led by partners and followed by implementation teams.

OWNERSHIP AND LEADERSHIP

A high pH firm must have leaders who are passionate about design. And the firm must address ownership and leadership in terms of roles, diversity, and transition.

It is critical that leaders have effective control over the strategy, direction, and behavior of the entity. The relationship between ownership and leadership is important in that regard. If there is a difference in interest or motivation between leaders and owners, there will likely be friction, which will be counterproductive as well as transparent to staff.

The simplest way to ensure this does not occur is to make the two synonymous: have the strongest leaders of the enterprise also be the majority owners, and have all owners active in the design practice. This approach aligns financial risk with both strategic decision making and tactical implementation. If these conditions are not met, then the design of ownership and leadership must be set up carefully to ensure that leaders have the authority to direct the practice. This requires a very artful governance structure to succeed. A divergence between owning and implementing divorces purpose from passion. Period.

Diversity is critical for any entity that is seeking high performance, especially if it is designing in a global environment. A narrow perspective simply will not achieve consistently relevant results. A passive diversity strategy will rarely accomplish adequate diversity change, so an active strategy is essential. An active strategy is difficult to design and manage. This is a part of firm design in which trial and error will be essential, and error management is a required art for success. Diversity in leadership includes ethnicity, gender, and age but also critical perspectives such as business and development, politics, and social science. All of that notwithstanding, leaders in a high pH firm will also be good generalist designers in whatever discipline they represent.

The issues of transition and renewal are important to the long-term success of a designing enterprise. Transition in leadership and ownership must be designed and supported by structure in a thoughtful and reasonably flexible way. There are numerous examples of once fine firms that deteriorated in slow and painful ways because leadership strength was not renewed, and in some cases leaders hung on to ownership well past their contribution to the purpose of the enterprise. It is important to develop an agreed strategy for mandatory renewal long before the time to implement it is near. An age-based mandatory sell down of ownership and or a mandatory review and adjustment of ownership are two strategies for this. The financial model for ownership transfer is critical to making this work. In a high pH entity, the value placed on ownership must be affordable by people who have not already established high net worth or the firm will never enjoy the diversity of high-performing youth.

To be successful in motivating the best talent in design, firm leaders must be design-focused and possess demonstrated design talent. But most of all, leaders must have the skill and style to draw out ideas and skill in others, helping them to develop talent and confidence. This is best accomplished by a selfless style of leadership that credits others for success and accepts responsibility for failures.

Ownership and Leadership at NBBJ

In the mid 1960s when I joined NBBJ, it was going through the ownership/leadership transition I described in the Introduction. This was a transition based on changing attitudes and aging senior partners but not particularly strategic. Nonetheless, the founding partners determined one way or another that they wanted the firm's legacy to continue, and they added a number of new partners to accomplish it. In a short period of time, the firm went from four partners to about 16. I was one of the partners swept into that net. And in the following couple of years, we added another few partners primarily through firm acquisitions. So with about 120 staff and 20 or so partners, we were top heavy and rather directionless. Out of frustration, four of us who were responsible for bringing in and overseeing most of the firm's work decided that the firm needed to be designed if we were to have any hope of achieving our goals of doing relevant, meaningful, top-quality architecture.

We went through a process by which we designed a new kind of structure. We consolidated direction setting in a smaller partnership group (five initially) who would stand behind that direction setting by taking responsibility for the financial risk of the firm, including providing the equity capital. Others who had been partners would remain principals in the firm with responsibility and relative autonomy for running their projects and would retain contract share of the firm's profit but have no responsibility for providing capital or for firm financial losses. We managed to convince the other partners that this was the best way forward, and in that process only one of the other partners decided to leave the firm (and later became a client).

As the firm grew, the partnership was expanded (of course the principal-ship was as well). And we were again faced with the issue of how many people can effectively participate in setting strategic direction. A group of five was highly effective, but even though there was diversity in personality and skill set, in the long run it was not diverse enough to deal with a globalizing practice adequately. It was gradually expanded.

By the time the number at the table reached 10, ideation sessions became noticeably less effective. By the time the number reached 12, the need for a structural modification was apparent. The modification designed at that time was to create a board structure to deal with strategy, limiting the board to five partners elected by the partnership. The board would also deal with financial issues of major magnitude and review budgets for recommendation to the partnership. Those actions felt to be particularly sensitive would be subject to ratification by the partnership as a whole.

NBBJ's Board is an essential part of our structure, enabling a reasonably sized strategic planning group and serving at the pleasure of the partnership, with key issues requiring partnership approval, therefore leaving the partners in ultimate control.

Partners who take on designated leadership roles in the firm (managing partners) must maintain a role in projects because we always want the firm led by active design-focused architects.

Another issue of concern to us as we looked ahead to a growing practice with new generations of leadership was how to ensure that the practice continued to evolve its leadership as a meritocracy that maintained the values we held dear. We saw very good firms suffering from a lack of leadership transition because they didn't have a financial mechanism or a methodology to ensure transition. As I indicated above, we strongly believe in alignment between active firm leadership and ownership.

To address this, we designed an approach that would make continuous transition in ownership relatively easy for both those relinquishing ownership and those acquiring it.

This approach recognized that the capital required to buy ownership is a significant barrier to many who should have it. Further, valuation of ownership is both contentious and subject to uncontrollable market conditions. We felt that a strong and continuous evolution of firm leadership was more important than maximizing payout to ourselves and future owners. We therefore set the value of the firm at 2.5 times actual earnings paid over five years. This means that the seller is paid half of the actual earnings on the share that he or she relinquishes for the five years following, and the buyer gets only half of those earnings for that five years. The advantage to the buyer is that he or she will not get trapped by an overvalued purchase, and the seller will still be motivated for the success of the firm. The advantage to the seller is that he or she benefits from earnings growth over those five years. (However, the seller is at risk if the firm tanks.) The voting right of the share immediately transfers to the buyer.

This approach allowed (and led to the expectation of) annual adjustments in ownership that accommodated new partners, retiring partners, and adjustments for long-term performance.

The firm capitalizes itself, annually setting the capital need and prorating that to ownership. To make that manageable for new partners, the firm set up a progressive loan system that allows partners to finance their capital at a reasonable rate (less than the firm paid them in interest on the same capital), but the percentage of their capital that they can finance declines every year so they have to put a significant portion of the earnings back into the firm until there is no loan against their capital account.

Further, to ensure that senior partners do not create undue obstacles to transition, they are automatically required to sell down their ownership by half between their 60th and 65th birthdays. After that, a mutually agreeable plan for continuing as an owner or not is negotiated between the partners. At the time I am writing this, five partners have left the partnership under this arrangement. It seems to work well and is generally perceived to be fair. One partner stayed on as an owner for a total of six years (and still works as a non-owning consultant); another chose to retire at 65. I stayed as a partner for two additional years and worked as a consultant for another year, and another partner became a non-partner outside board member for three years. Under this sellout mechanism, a partner still has ownership interest (non-voting except on issues affecting ownership) for the five-year sell down period. The age for the sell down, originally set almost 20 years ago, was reset to age 62 to 67 in 2010, and it should be revisited every 10 years or so.

Diversity in age (currently 39 to 67) has been achieved. Diversity in gender is not so balanced (three women to 12 men). Nationalities represented include partners born in Eastern Europe, Cuba, and Asia as well as the United States. There are an interior designer, landscape architect, construction manager, and accountant among the partners.

Ownership and Leadership in Danish Firms

3XN is owned by five male architect partners in two age groups, roughly 15 years apart. The partners lead the firm and determine strategy as described above, so there is clear alignment between active practicing leaders and ownership. One of the partners is CEO.

The firm's board of three outsiders and three partners is largely advisory and a strong networking tool. There is no defined ownership transition plan in place.

Arkitema has a limited liability partnership with 13 male architect partners, all active in the practice. The firm has a non-architect managing director and a four-person board with two outside members and two partners. Again, ownership and leadership are reasonably aligned, but there is no apparent transition strategy in place, and the imminent retirement of the founding partners all at the same time is a remarkable event.

BIG is owned by six male architect partners and two associate partners. One of the associate partners is a woman who is managing director. There is no defined ownership transition plan in place, and it is not yet on the radar screen.

C.F. Moller is a partnership of eight architects and an accountant, two women and seven men, one Italian born, one German born, and the rest Danish. One partner is son of the founder. The partners are all active in practice and lead the firm. There is no apparent transition contract, though the firm obviously has negotiated transition through two generations without trauma.

Henning Larsen's six partners own and lead the firm, and there are eight other leaders who hold an economic interest in the firm as associate partners. One of six partners is a woman (and CEO), and two of the eight associate partners are women. Strategy is set by this leader owner group. The firm is well into the transition from the founder and the second generation now owns a majority. There are specifics of a transition in place, including an age-related sell down requirement. The current board structure is large and felt to be unwieldy because of its makeup. Of a total of eight, one is a partner, three are outside members, and four are selected by firm staff. I am told that this is likely to change soon.

Schmidt Hammer Lassen is a five male architect partnership, all active in leading the practice. There are three associate partners, one of whom is a woman. There is a non-partner CEO who is a woman. Business management is led by the CEO Bente Damgaard, and creative management is led by partner Bjarne Hammer. The board of three outside members (all closely aligned to areas of SHL's practice) and two founding partners is very influential in strategy thinking and direction setting. There is no defined ownership transition plan in place.

PLACE

The workplace is one of the most tangible expressions of the values of a culture. The place for high design performance must not only enable it, but it must proclaim it as a belief system in the aesthetics of place as well as in its function and humanity.

Although there is not a comprehensive research basis for this, designers, and particularly architects, should be aware of the influence of the work environment on behavior and creative performance. Nonetheless, many design workplaces seem to place most of their emphasis on being a showroom for aesthetic attitude. While clients and potential clients are keenly interested in their designers' own space, those that are seeking a high-performance design are more likely impressed by an environment that reflects a high-performance culture than one that reflects only a showplace for design aesthetic.

A high pH space is all about the work. It is as non-hierarchical as the culture it supports. It is open and flexible, with individual, small, and large group and team-based spaces. The work in progress is apparent, including all of the versions of ideation: verbal, symbolic, representational, modeling in all its forms. It utilizes the tools of daylight, view, color, texture, sound, and smell to aid performance. It makes an interesting environment for celebration (and sometimes grieving). It reflects the values espoused by the firm, such as economy of resource utilization, sustainability, and affordability. And, of course, it must have a deeply inspiring aesthetic quality.

Place at NBBJ

One of the more transformative events at NBBJ was when the Seattle office relocated to Pioneer Square in Seattle in 1983. This move was from a hierarchical, rabbit warren environment to an almost totally open one in a building with high floor-to-floor dimensions typical of early 20th-century warehouses. The design process for this space was rapid (to beat a tax incentive deadline) but nonetheless pushed on many reorganizational concepts. We partners, however, hung on stubbornly to our private office prerogatives, so there were corner offices on each of the floors. However, after moving in and experiencing the team and studio camaraderie this environment provided, partners soon felt disconnected and left out, more than slightly pompous, and a little silly. The partners soon took open workstations with their project teams, and these corner offices became conference rooms (though retaining the possibly satirical conference room nomenclature of "2 Partners" (second floor), "3 Partners" (third floor), etc. This new environment was the incubator for our studio system, which was adopted firm-wide within a couple of years, and it helped enable many of the cultural changes that have shaped NBBJ. It had a gathering space that all 300-plus people could squeeze into (standing) for presentation, dialogue, and celebration. Standing also encouraged a concise presentation style, which itself was a benefit. That office environment was mentioned by a number of clients in debriefings on why we won their work.

Each time we have moved or renovated an office space, it has provided the opportunity to reexamine the way we work and make changes that have continued to shape the practice. When our Los Angeles office moved to an old film studio in Marina Del Rey, the model shop became a major focus, and we greatly increased the amount of physical modeling and prototyping in the practice. When we again moved the Seattle office in 2007, this time to a new building we designed, we knew a lot more about how to use various gathering spaces, and we had a much higher regard for physical modeling, which now is prominent in the center of our space. The sustainable focus of the building (LEED Silver building, Gold interior, but more important, meeting the 2030 Challenge) with great daylight and natural ventilation has inspired staff. When we relocated our New York office to 2 Rector Street, we added big screens to team gathering places. All of our offices are open space, and in each is a large gathering place available for full staff gatherings, and they all are good party spaces.

Place in Danish Firms

All six Danish firms have open office environments in the offices I visited. Partners shared open space with the teams with which they worked. All of them were in spaces where the action of design was visible to visitors. Products, models, and drawings of work in progress were apparent as well as more permanent display of past work. One notable difference between American firms and most of these Danish firms is the importance and prominence of the canteen, where most of the staff have lunch (a part of the social contract). This creates a staff mixing and sense of camaraderie not often enjoyed by American firms.

3XN is in an open planned, no-private-office environment in two spatially connected stories of waterfront loft under a double pitched roof. The teams work in open spaces with nearby access to open team critique space.

Arkitema in Aarhus occupies three transparent stories plus a penthouse wrapped around a three-story skylit atrium in a building they designed. It has a number of transparent but glass-enclosed as well as open meeting spaces.

BIG is in an open, high-bay warehouse space with lots of accessible storage for their accumulated models. Both open and enclosed but transparent meeting spaces near team workspace enables easy team critiques.

C.F.Moller in Aarhus is in the top five floors plus an added penthouse of a 12-story building. The space is open stories linked by a single grand staircase that traverses all of them. Teams are in open space with nearby semi-open critique spaces.

Henning Larsen in Copenhagen is in the top two stories of a former department store, with two open floors around a two-story skylit atrium. Each of the floors is home to one of their geographic units (Scandinavian and international).There are open critique spaces on each level as well as transparent conference spaces.

Schmidt Hammer Lassen's space in Aarhus is an open and transparent space with a prominent model shop, open critique spaces, and open transparent partner workstations at the periphery. In Copenhagen they are in an open incubator space in the meat packing district.

6

TAKEAWAYS

I set out to make a case for raising architects' design aspirations to pursuit of high-performance design, a triple bottom line approach (people/social, planet/environment, financial/ efficiency and profit) to the changes we design for our environment. The important reason for that is a moral one: We must get the most benefit of any change we design into the environment and make the most of the resources we commit to accomplish it. If we don't, we are not justified in denying those same resources to worthier endeavors. This is a moral mandate. As Alain de Botton says "To care deeply about a field that achieves so little, and yet consumes so many of our resources, forces us to admit to a disturbing, even degrading lack of aspiration."[74]

A secondary reason is that if we don't optimize the way we as a profession (design) and an industry (design and construction) deliver projects, we will lose our privileged position to perform this role, and the world will suffer environments assembled almost exclusively from a pragmatic and narrowly focused bias.

And, finally, a tertiary and self-serving reason (for Western architects) is that we will lose our competitive creative advantage if we don't carry our work beyond the realm of inspiring form and incorporate total system performance as well.

Most successful industries and institutions have continuously rethought and reinvented not only their processes but the relevance of their product and their *raison d'être* as well. The design professions have not done this convincingly ... and need to.

I define high-performance design as design that:

- Awakens and inspires the human spirit
- Transforms the user enterprise to a higher level of performance
- Makes the place (or object) better than what went before it, including the context in which it resides

[74] De Botton, Alain, *The Architecture of Happiness*, Random House Vintage Books, New York 2006, p. 20.

- Is accomplished with the minimum, essential, and sustainable resources
- Is affordable to the user enterprise and to society (in all resources, including time and money)

That includes three criteria not applied to recognition of great architecture by such awards as the Pritzker Prize, the Mies van der Rohe Award for European Architecture, or even the BusinessWeek/Architectural Record Awards (a jury I served on in 1999). The difference is the both/and of design spirit plus human performance plus economy of means and affordability, the latter two being basically absent or unrecognized in these award programs. For high-quality design to become a more dominant presence in our environment, it must address the broad spectrum of need with great economy of means. That is high-performance design.

This level of design can only be accomplished consistently by a close and effective collaboration of a diverse team of designers. Also, it can best be implemented through a close collaboration of owner/users, designers, and fabricator/builders.

To achieve this, design entities must thoughtfully design themselves to achieve high design performance, a characteristic that I label high pH because it requires a combination of great people and effective habitat. The design of such a firm must focus on its projects as the *raison d'être* for every aspect of it. Designing and building such a practice requires focused effort on a continuous basis. It is worth the effort because that is what it takes to produce consistent outcomes in design and because it is an exhilarating way to practice design.

I reviewed six leading and very creative Danish design firms because I think Danish firms' performance on the world stage is remarkable and that maybe it is their national ethos that gives them an edge in pursuing high-performance design. I believe that more than ever now. These firms were able to create collaborative creative environments with less conscious effort than firms in other countries because of the cultural base they start from. They have a societal bias for both design excellence and economy of means, and they have a strong social conscience — several of the important ingredients for high design performance. And these six firms all have produced high-performance design. While none of them have all of the characteristics I find essential, they are all, to varying degrees, well positioned to become high pH firms it if they so choose.

In designing and implementing a high pH firm:

- People selection starts with firm leaders who complement each other with diverse skills and perspective as well as with creative tension and shared passion, values, and agreed purpose.
- All other staff, whether they are designers or not, must be selected with these same characteristics as criteria.
- Habitat for creative performance includes culture, approach, and structure.

Culture is formed by living a set of values, maintaining a clear sense of worthy purpose, and by being inclusive and communicative. It is kept vital by continuous curiosity and willingness to risk change.

An approach for high-performance design must ensure breadth of discovery and ideation and effectiveness of implementation. This requires constant exploration and design of processes, both project-specific and practice-wide. And it includes continuous stimulation of the creative process.

Structure is critical to enable effective focus on design, but very often it is set up as though design should serve the structure, with accounting systems geared to generate banking ratios rather than informing design, for instance. Structure can and must be designed to partner with project teams in the creative process. Support staff must feel a part of the design effort.

Becoming a high pH design entity requires a change process initially, followed by a continuous pursuit of the ideal.

It is very tempting as a designer to say: "This takes too much time ... just design it! Spend the time there." Understandable, but without the rigor to design the way we pursue it, design almost always falls short of what it could have, should have been. I think that is not just amoral, it is immoral.

If a majority of design were pursued on the basis of high-performance design, the payoff to society would be enormous. The savings and value generated would be more than enough to end global poverty and place the planet on a sustainable energy, water, and food regimen. That's right, the stakes are huge. And it would be pretty damn satisfying to designers.

POSTSCRIPT

I have described a lot of my experience at NBBJ in writing this book, and of course the firm has not been idle during the time of this writing. The studio and markets structure continue to be tweaked, an even stronger commitment has been made to a single digital platform, and great progress has been made in implementing transformational change through architecture. The firm has successfully implemented a new operations start-up service for clients with new and transformative buildings; it has pushed parametric design effectively into the realms of human experience and into economy of means. It has merged with very fine firms in Boston (Chan Krieger Sieniewics) and San Francisco (Fisher-Friedman Associates) and has added a partner in Los Angeles. I am fortunate to be invited to consult with the firm just enough to keep me in the loop on interesting aspects of strategy and markets. In my view, the firm is rigorously pursuing the quest that began many years ago and is continuing to discover new challenges to address. The legacy of the firm continues because the leaders were selected for the right reasons and were engaged in the practice in the right way. About that I have a most embarrassing sense of pride.

NOTES

The Danish Firms

My interest in Danish firms began with exposure to a couple of firms when I was researching health care design in Europe in the late 1960s and was reinforced much later when competing with some of them for major projects in invited competitions. I also was intrigued by reading an account of the way Niels Bohr, the Danish Nobel Prize winner in physics, collaboratively ran his Physics Institute in Copenhagen and the Copenhagen conferences on quantum mechanics from 1929 until the start of World War II, which evolved the generally accepted Copenhagen interpretation of quantum mechanics. In both cases, he was known for encouraging the active participation of a diverse group of minds, including young students, with "equal treatment for ideas originating from the youngest or the oldest, the fresh Ph.D. or the Nobel Prize winner."[75] This, along with the other indications of a collaborative ethos mentioned in footnotes in the Preface and the start of Chapter 5, made me believe that Danish design firms have an inherent mastery of a collaborative approach.

I engaged with six Danish firms, all included on the ArcSpace Web site. I visited their offices, had discussions with one or more partners and usually some of their staff, and I visited some of their projects. I had been a finalist in design competitions in Norway and Iceland in which several of these firms competed, and one of them won in both cases. I had also met some of them at a discussion on international practice hosted for NBBJ by Kent Martinussen and the Danish Architectural Center in 2008.

---

75 Segre, Gino, *Faust in Copenhagen: A Struggle for the Soul of Physics*, New York, Penguin Group, 2007, p. 29.

3XN

Three graduates of the Arhus school, all named Nielsen but not related, started this firm in 1986. Two of them have since left the firm, which is now headed by Kim Herforth Nielsen and four other partners. This is currently a first-generation firm beginning to think about the second.

The firm has offices in Copenhagen and Aarhus and a staff of about 100.Major projects include Museum of Liverpool, Muziekgebouw (music hall in Amsterdam), and Saxo Bank headquarters in Copenhagen. Two of its transformative landmark projects are Orestad College, which won the Best Building in Scandinavia Award in 2007, and the Green Pavilion in the Sculpture Park of the Louisiana Museum, which won the JEC Innovation Award 2010.

Photo by Adam Mørk

The Blue Planet
Denmark for The Blue Planet Building Foundation (a joint venture of Realdania Foundation, Knud Højgaards Foundation & Tårnby Municipality)
3XN Architects

Arkitema

Five architecture students set up an architectural collective in 1969, which became Arkitektgruppen Aarhus in 1970. By 2002 it was known as Arkitema. Now with 13 partners and a total staff of around 160, the firm has offices in Aarhus, Copenhagen, and Stockholm and had a Beijing office until 2009. It is pretty much into its second generation, though most founding partners were still active when I visited the firm in early 2010.

It has a product design group Arkitema Design; a construction prefabrication group, Arkitema Prefab; a sustainability consultancy, Arkitema Energy; and Arkitema Planning & Landscape. The firm is known for its innovative approach to process, which it calls "sensmaking" and for innovation in construction approach.

Recent projects of note include the Sluseholmen Canal Community in Copenhagen and the restoration of Frederik VIII's Mansion.

Photos by permission of Arkitema

Arkitema House
Aarhus, Denmark
Akitema Architects

BIG

Bjarke Ingels founded the Bjarke Ingels Group after a brief stint in a partnership with fellow students, then working for Rem Koolhaas' firm the Office for Metropolitan Architecture and joint work with a colleague from that experience, Julien de Smedt, in a firm known as PLOT. BIG is a first-generation firm with six partners, two associate partners, and a total staff of about 80. The firm is located in Copenhagen. It is part of a broader design entity called KiBiSi, with Kilo Design and Skibsted Ideation, for the purpose of broad-ranging design application from transportation to life-style. BIG is known for socially and economically innovative housing like The Mountain in Orestad, winner of the 2009 Forum AID Award as well as a ULI award. More recently, it has won acclaim for institutional work such as the design-competition-winning Danish Maritime Museum in Helsingor.

The Mountain
restad, Denmark
BIG-The Bjarke Ingels Group

Photo by Jakob Galit

C.F. Moller

C.F. Moller Architects is one of the oldest practices in Scandinavia. It was founded by Christian Frederik Moller in 1924 in Aarhus. C.F. Moller is in its third generation.

Currently there are nine partners and slightly over 300 staff. Offices are in Aarhus, Copenhagen, Aalborg, Oslo, London, and Stockholm.

Among its recent notable works are the Darwin Center at the Natural History Museum, London, and the design-competition-winning Akershus University Hospital in Norway. The firm's product designs (C.F. Moller Design) have also won numerous awards.

Photos by Torben Eskerod — copyright Natural History Museum.

Second phase of the Darwin Centre
London
C.F. Moller Architects

Henning Larsen

Founded in 1959 by the firm's namesake, the firm is now in the hands of a second generation of six partners and eight associate partners. The total staff is about 130, and the firm is located in Copenhagen.

Key recent work includes the Opera House in Copenhagen and the Reykjavik Concert & Conference Centre.

Photo by Adam Mørk

Copenhagen Opera
Denmark
Henning Larsen Architects

Schmidt Hammer Lassen

The three partners founded this practice in 1986 and have since taken on two additional partners. The firm is just now exploring the second generation and has three associate partners. The total staff is currently about 140, and they have offices in Aarhus, Copenhagen, Oslo, London, and Shanghai.

Significant projects include the Royal Library, Copenhagen (known as the Black Diamond), the ARos Museum, Aarhus, and the Katuaq Culture Centre in Greenland.

Photo courtesy of Schmidt Hammer Lassen

ARos Museum
Aarhus, Denmark
Schmidt Hammer Lassen Architects

NBBJ LEGACY

The following is a paper I presented to my partners at their request in our 2005 annual meeting that has been shared with every new partner since. It deals with the legacy of the firm from a long-term perspective. Some of these thoughts have been covered in the text of the book.

Values in a Design Practice: 40 Years at NBBJ

Jim Jonassen delivered to NBBJ partners, Scotland, October 2005

Purpose

This is to provide some insight into what has happened to shape the values inherent in what we now (2005) think of as the NBBJ culture. This is my perspective, and of course many of the people who participated in this experience over the years will have their own perhaps similar, perhaps different view.

I joined NBBJ in 1965. At that time the firm was already 22 years old, and the predecessor firms that founded it had histories going back as much as several decades prior to that. At the point that I came into the firm there were three transformations going on at once:

1. A shift from the founding generation to a legacy firm (motivated by fairness to participants as much as by a need to capture equity)
2. A shift from pure profession to profession as business (to stay in business you had to control your cost structure and create systems for marketing and doing work and getting paid)
3. A shift from a delivery-oriented design firm to a design-oriented firm good at delivery (Bill Bain was leading this)

Values that were apparent at the time, made large by Perry Johanson more than anyone, included:

- Respect for differences in skills at the partner level (i.e. design, promotion, delivery, operations).

- Fairness to individuals but with overriding importance of the legacy.
- Willingness by individual partners to take on those things that the firm needed and give up things that were not in the firm's best interests.
- Essential equality as partners.

These values were heavily imprinted by him on most of us who worked with him for any length of time.

From Founders to Legacy

The methods of succession were perhaps a little puzzling, but remember this was largely an experiment in those days.

- **Economics of Transition**

  The economics of this transition were based on a commissioned study (Booz Allen, I think) and then what seemed like the fairest and most reasonable path was chosen. This was a five times three-year average multiple of earnings borne by the buyer, owed directly to the seller. In that era buyouts were being structured from 8 to 11 times earnings, so this seemed like a legacy deal indeed.

  When a couple of back-to-back downturn years occurred, this buyout burden proved infeasible, particularly for rapidly rising partners. The firm leadership restructured in a way that was fair to all — the firm taking on the debt and restructuring future buyouts.

  After trying several approaches for a few years, including nothing-in, nothing-out (eminently unfair to practice builders and great incentive to hang on to power), the firm leadership settled on a prospective approach that tied buy-out to actual future performance, reducing buyers' risk and increasing sellers' motivation for future firm success. The value was then set at a modest 2.5 times (prospective) earnings and a buyout mechanism that gave the buyer immediate earnings and made the debt a firm responsibility.

  Still later it was decided, initially as a gentleperson's agreement, that to ensure constant renewal of the firm, a stipulated sell-down procedure would be followed, reducing ownership by half (in the five fiscal years following a partner's 60th birthday) and at the end of that period a separation or a mutually agreed continuance would take place. This has been followed for a number of years and was more recently incorporated in the partnership agreements.

- **Partnership Succession**

The succession selection seemed hurried; perhaps it had waited a little too long. A lot of people were selected in a short period of time (12 new partners added to the total in a nine-year period which included several retirements). The succession to partnership in the '70s was a bit of a sweep of likely internal candidates (I was swept in in 1970), followed by promotion of leaders of internal companies (BSD Business Space Design, MPS, CPM Cost Management and Planning) and firm acquisitions (Godwin Bohm, Maynard Partch) each of which added partners. The strategic "direction" at the time was skill and geographic diversity but without a cohesive strategy about what a partner was, or what roles and responsibilities were.

It soon became apparent that 18 partners (not all of whom had strategic or practice building skills and each with a feeling of direction-giving entitlement) was not a working structure, and that design of the design firm was needed. When a few of us took initiative to start that design it was obvious that it had to start at what was then thought of as the "top" and fairness of the process was a paramount concern.

- **Redesign the Design Firm**

So the firm was redesigned with a small partnership to determine future direction. We wanted a balance to make it both fair and attractive to other essential leaders and to those existing partners who would not be partners in the newly designed firm. We created a structure where partners who would set future direction would also hold the liability for that and (later) capitalize it, and principals (other essential leaders) would be spared liability risk but still share in profits. We were careful to settle amicably with all of the partners who were not included in the restructured partnership and all but one of them stayed with the firm as principals (and that one later became a client). I think we succeeded in the goal of being fair and making it a win/win situation.

From time to time we have subsequently had to terminate both partners and principals, but have always tried to make each of these partings fair and respectful, financially and otherwise, always seeking a win/win proposition.

This is not only the right thing to do but I think in the long run has always been beneficial to the firm. It is always the right time to do the right thing.

A number of times it has become apparent that a change in roles between partners would benefit the firm and in almost every case it has been done voluntarily with a minimum of fuss:

Perry Johanson voluntarily stepped down as managing partner in favor of David Hoedemaker in 1975 when we needed strong spiritual leadership for design

- David voluntarily stepped down as CEO of NBBJ West for me in 1983 (Bohm was CEO in the East), when we were challenged for financial rigor and needed restructuring.
- In 1986 Dave stepped aside as managing partner in favor of Friedl (who continued as CEO East) when we needed a business perspective unifying East and West.
- I stepped aside as CEO West, and Friedl as CEO East when it was apparent that we needed to develop younger CEOs in Scott and Neil.
- Neil stepped aside when the One Firm initiative restructured to a firm core team.

This ethic is reinforced and enabled by the attitude of essential equality of partners. It has been a key to the firm's success. Very few partners along the way were unable to cope with this level of change, and left the firm, most under positive circumstance.

Shift From Pure Profession to Profession as Business

This change manifested itself in two significant ways:

- Change from "1/3 for doing the work, 1/3 for keeping the office open, 1/3 for the partners" to a complex, competitive, and regulated cost and compensations structure.
- Change from the majority of work walking in the door based on relationships to the majority of work being openly competed for (even though relationships are still critical).

The firm had operated for 20 years in an environment that had changed very slowly, but by the '60s change was moving at a visible pace.

- **Business Structure**

  The firm adjusted to this new business environment by adding skills and trying a number of structures. It was a great laboratory to learn how to recognize need for change and to develop alternatives for coping at worst, leading on average, and transforming at best. A number of accounting experts were tried and it took some sorting to find those whose client- and staff-focused values matched those of the high standards that the partners believed in.

  The studio structure which started as a one studio experiment in 1983 became a model which was developed to align fiscal and professional responsibility with serving the client's needs (and to provide a wide open check on accountability). This has continuously been redefined as new lessons are learned.

- **Markets Structure**

  Development of a markets structure began by recognizing that architects' communication was not particularly effective with the audiences key to selecting architects. There was a step-by-step learning of better ways to communicate, of learning the importance of understanding client's needs, of shaping designs to client (and community) needs, and being what you are selling. All of this was a continuous classroom of values and ethics. The studio system was directly aimed at stopping the bait-and-switch sales ethic of many firms at the time and when first implemented was a painful step backward in short-term markets success (but we believed in its long-term value to clients).

Shift from Delivery to Design

The firm was highly regarded in its ability to deliver a sound product with predictable cost and good quality design. There was a desire to seek greatness in design manifested by Bill Bain (probably reflecting values also held by his father) and supported by Perry Johanson. The pathway for this started in the early '60s when Bill came back from Cornell and was in full swing when I joined the firm in 1965. Young architects like Hoedemaker (Yale), Winkelmann

(Yale), Sowder (Ecole Des Beaux Arts) and me (Columbia) were being given great projects to work on, with high responsibility and a great need to develop a base of followers from an existing cadre of delivery-focused architects and a growing cadre of new hires. This was a very interesting learning experience in leveraging leadership from a position of low experience and technical skill levels. In the process we each learned that good design doesn't get realized just because it is good; it takes a complete and focused effort by a complete team. Those who survived became pretty strong and understanding of the value of different skills and collaboration.

This time was a learning laboratory about design for impact on client's performance. For me this started with Battelle Richland under Bill's guidance where we created a desert oasis environment for staff, and it continued through a series of projects where I was introduced to a program methodology based on aggressive curiosity about a client's goals and operations and their relationship to surrounding communities. This lead to a series of projects that broke new ground:

- Heath Building that focused on matching module to market in a new market to the region (and daylight corridors)
- Wenatchee Medical Center (un-built) that was the first design for a true medical shopping center, including underground service spine and a total incremental growth strategy
- Swedish Master Plan that created an integrated retail face with the community, first to orient all patient rooms to a view, found and declared the natural urban site boundaries, functional zoning
- Mayo Clinic Surgery (also a lesson in joint venturing) in which we developed a new operational model which drove the planning

That period shaped a focus on looking at all aspects of the clients' situation and finding those things that were most important to push. This has lead to a balance of left and right brained thinking which put us in the forefront of design ideas in health care:

- Separating building types by use (tri partite zoning) in the '70s
- Healing/performance design addressed in the late '80s (Children's San Diego as poster child)

- Health system rationalization (Good Health System) early '90s
- Autogenesic system for change response in the late '90s (from Fukui to Banner)

Rick Buckley picked up strongly on content-based design and helped push it to a dominant approach in the firm in the years before he died.

Carrying on Firm Legacy

The development of a legacy firm has been about building a value system, an approach, a culture, a track record of project work that enhances life and performance. The goal is an entity that people are proud of and want to spend their careers in. Ours has been of a practice that addresses all aspects of life, not equally but in a balance appropriate to the situation.

- ***Value System***

  Our value system while initially shaped by the firm's founders has been continuously refined and adjusted by our actions. As Bronowski says;

  > " ... that modern school of historians who believe that we read principles into history after the event, but that at the time we act by expediency. All acts of state ... are particular acts; they do not conform to principles but rather, one by one, combine to form the principles which we then discover in them."*

  So in many cases we were making decisions about what seemed right and in hindsight finding consistency a defining principle. The voluntary actions of partners to change roles, the concerns for fairness in sharing both credit for work and profits from it, concerns which were debated long and hard, resulted in defined principles and expected behaviors. This is something that will continue to define what the firm is. Our concern for clients, their communities, and for the planet, while inherent in the founder's views have been tested and reshaped by a multitude of both positive and not so positive experiences, many requiring difficult judgments to be made. There has been no perfection in this, and we must constantly face the challenge of our own human frailties. The judgments that you make will continue to define the firm.

- *Vision*

The vision for the firm, that declaration of aspiration that helps guide these judgments, has been a key to our success. In the '70s we struggled in an emulation of what we saw as great in a few other practices (the problem-seeking mentality of CRS, the multi-locational excellence, consistency, autonomy of SOM). We struggled further as we began to realize that the balance to address all aspects of project success was a different, and more difficult aspiration than we saw others pursuing.

In the late '70s, early '80s we tried expressing specific attributes we wanted to achieve as our vision (remember the wine bottles at my desk):

- Beautiful buildings and environments
- Personal, professional and financial satisfaction
- Satisfied customers
- Contribution to a better society

These were relatively short lived, as we realized that kind of incrementalism wasn't satisfying our aspirations.

In the late '80s (1987?) we determined that nothing less big, bold, and hairy than being the "best design firm in the world" would get us there. This took two steps, however. First we said "best large design firm in the world" thinking that we needed to define the difference in what we thought best meant as a complete addressing of issues versus the boutique or star firm focus on aesthetics and form alone.

But in a couple of years we got past this hesitancy about our definition and dropped "large."

The immediate and continued debate about the meaning of this vision, reinforced by mostly consistent behaviors has kept the firm focused in a powerful way. In the early 2000s we further refined brand by adopting and expanding on an idea initially expressed in the planning practice: "Artists of change: fearlessly creative, collaboratively developed and intelligently realized."

Even more recently the acknowledgement that the value that we are seeking to add for our clients and their communities is a transformational one has raised the bar in both our aspiration and our understanding of it. This continual reevaluating what society needs in "the best design firm" keeps the quest alive and well. The next important steps may be a more specific approach to the needs of a global society.

- ***Culture***

We have learned that culture is something that forms itself but is enabled and shaped by the environment you create and the judgments you make about people.

In our case we have attempted to focus debate and performance on the issues of our practice, not on the personalities. That enables open discussion of the most difficult of issues with a maximum of openness to ideas and a minimum of personal defensiveness.

The studio culture was created to enable people to have an immediate and effective say in shaping their practice and projects, and sharing in rewards. The specifics of the studio model have been continuously refined and sometimes redefined as the practice has matured. Recent changes have focused on enabling cross studio projects in a global practice environment. Our current goal of a global practice in which local people are partners is an extension of our cultural ideal to the global scale.

Another success of our culture has been a high level of openness which leads to a high level of trust. Many of the failures we have had have been when we were not open and allowed people to become politicized rather than issue focused.

"Who does not trust enough will not be trusted." *Lao Tzu, Tao Te Ching*

- ***Approach***

We saw a failure in approach in the first transition years of the partnership, when there wasn't a balance in addressing all aspects of the work, and variously only design, or only marketing, or only delivery were satisfied. It was a huge firm shaping realization that the unevenness of those approaches never provided truly transcending work.

Valuing all ideas combined with the leadership to select and shape the best has lead to a highly collaborative approach.

The idea of specifically designing the approach to each project around the client and its issues, the strengths and aspirations of the design team and the regulatory and construction environment, while it was invented around a specific project need, has become a valuable and still unique tool for success.

Our enterprise discovery approach had its seeds in the early days of admiration for CRS but has grown way beyond that through our embracing a multitude of disciplines and integrated design. Dallam's recent push of the black box, blue sky approach is a great example of this.

- ***Project Track Record***

  Our projects have been on a continuous improvement path for as long as I have been with the firm. That path has pushed our work up the relative scale of excellence and made us credible contenders to achieve our aspiration of best design firm. Our most recent work includes that with the highest level of content and richness of form, with the highest performance outcome.

  This has been a tremendous push which has often been challenged by expediency and occasional myopia toward our vision. Further progress is progressively more difficult and more than ever can only be achieved by greatness in every aspect of the project from marketing (client discovery and development, expectation setting) design (content appropriate and rich, form inspiring and sustainable) delivery (high quality and efficient), and total outcome (performance and experience).

SUMMARY

The continuous building of a firm legacy never stops and it demands both a long view and a fair bit of selflessness. It always demands making hard decisions about what will be best to advance that legacy:

- decisions about bringing in new talent that may be difficult but add something needed,
- about trying people in roles and helping them succeed but if necessary helping them exit,

- about creating a vision for where and how the firm can best create for society,
- and acting consistently on that vision, especially when it is a hard thing to do,
- and very importantly about doing a good job of replacing your own skills in the firm with someone even better for the times.

I have long admired this quote from an unknown source (given to me by John Savo)

> "We are now, and always will be, in a stage of becoming, of trying to fulfill our changing dreams and aspirations. What we can accomplish at one stage of life is different from what we can handle at another. The more willing we are to shed another skin, the more centered, stable, and spirit-filled we'll become."— Unknown[76]

And on a lighter side we should keep in mind that:

"Sacred cows make the tastiest hamburger." — *Abbie Hoffman*

*(J. Bronowski & Bruce Mazlish, *The Western Intellectual Tradition from Leonardo to Hegel)*

[76] This has since been identified for me by Hugh Hochberg as from *A Woman's Spirit: More Meditations for Women* by Karen Casy, 1994.

ACKNOWLEDGEMENTS

I owe the inspiration to write this book to all of my colleagues at NBBJ over the now 47 years that I have been associated with the firm. Our sharing of the quest for high-performance design has made a great professional life. I am particularly indebted to Bill Bain, David Hoedemaker, and Friedl Bohm for initiating this quest with me.

I am deeply grateful to my partner in life, Marilyn Jonassen, for her encouragement and commentary on the process of authorship.

My Danish colleagues were most generous of their time, insights, and comments on a draft. I particularly want to thank Kent Martinussen of the Danish Architectural Centre for his sponsorship of the NBBJ dialogue with Danish firms several years ago, which enabled some of my early contacts and for his encouragement and advice on the book.

Colleagues in the firms I reviewed who were delightfully open and generous with their time include Kim Herfoth Nielsen and Lise Roland Johansen from 3XN, Lars Due from Arkitema, Bjarke Ingells and Kai-Uwe Bergmann from BIG, Tom Danielsen from C.F. Moller, Mette Kinne Frandsen from Henning Larsen, and Bjarne Hammer and Marlene Morup Damgaard-Sorensen from Schmidt Hammar Lassen.

My Danish cousins, Iversens and Jonasens, were great company and very helpful and supportive of me during my stays in Denmark.

I was helped immeasurably by the insightful, challenging and supportive critiques of an early manuscript by Ralph Hawkins, Hugh Hochberg, Steve McConnell, Scott Simpson, and Scott Wyatt. While many of their comments influenced my thinking and are reflected in the text, none of them would likely agree with the entire outcome.

I thank my partners at NBBJ for their financial support, Jim Cramer and Jane Gaboury for their editorial and publishing assistance, and Austin Cramer for layout design.

BIBLIOGRAPHY

Adams,James J., *Conceptual Blockbusting: A Guide to Better Ideas Third Edition*, New York, Addison-Wesley Publishing, 1986

Amabile, Teresa M., *Creativity in Context*, Boulder Colorado, Westview Press, 1996

Anderson, Harold H. editor, *Creativity and its Cultivation*, New York, Harper & Row 1959

Architecture for Humanity, ed. *Design Like You Give a Damn*, New York, Metropolis Books, 2006

Arup, Ove, *The Key Speech*, delivered July 9, 1970, to his partners at a meeting in Winchester, England, available on the Arup Web site *www.arup.com*

Bjarke Ingalls Group, *Yes is More*, Cologne, Evergreen, 2009

Brownell, Blaine, ed., *Transmaterial: A catalog of materials that redefine our physical environment*, New York: Princeton Architectural Press, 2004

Christakis, Nicholas A. and James H. Fowler, *Connected: The surprising Power of Our Social Networks and How They Shape Our Lives*, New York,Little, Brown and Company, 2009

De Bono, Edward, *De Bono's Thinking Course*, New York, Facts On File, 1982

De Bono, Edward, *Lateral Thinking: Creativity Step by Step*, New York Harper & Row, 1970

De Bono, Edward, New Think, New York, Avon Books 1967

De Bono, Edward, *Six Thinking Hats*, Boston, Little Brown & Co 1985

De Botton, Alain, *The Architecture of Happiness*, Random House Vintage Books, New York 2000

Gawande, Atul, *The Checklist Manifesto: How to Get Things Right*, New York, Metropolitan Books, 2009

Gordon, W., *Synectics: The Development of Creative Capacity*, New York Harper & Row, 1961

Grudin, Robert, *The Grace of Great Things: Creativity and Innovation,* New York: Ticknor & Fields, 1990

Hara, Kenya, *Designing Design*, Baden, Switzerland, Lars Muller Publishers, 2007

Hirshberg, Jerry, *The Creative Priority: Driving Innovative Business in the Real World,* New York, Harper Collins 1998

Finch, Paul, Preface to *investigate ask tell draw build*, 3XN architects, London, Black dog publishing 2007

Jackson, P., & S. Messick, *The person, the product and the response: Conceptual problems in the assessment of creativity, Journal of Personality,* 1965

Kelley, Tom, *The Art of Innovation: Lessons in Creativity from IDEO, America's Leading Design Firm,* New York, Doubleday 2001

Kennedy, Michael N., *Product Development for the Lean Enterprise*, Richmond Virginia: Oaklea Press 2003

Kotter, John P., *Leading Change: Why Transformation Efforts Fail*, Boston: Harvard Business Review, March-April 1995

Levitin, Daniel J., *This is your Brain on Music: The Science of a Human Obsession*, New York, Penguin Group, 2006

Martin, Roger, *The Design of Business*, Boston, Harvard Business Press, 2009

Martin, Roger, *The Opposable Mind*, Boston, Harvard Business Press, 2007

Medina, John, *Brain Rules; 12 Principles for Surviving and Thriving at Work, Home, and School*, Seattle, Pear Press, 2008

NBBJ, *Change Design: Conversations about Architecture as the Ultimate Business Tool,* Atlanta, Greenway Communications, 2006

Pink, Daniel H., *A Whole New Mind: Why Right Brains will Rule the Future,* New York, Riverhead Books, 2005

Sachs, Jeffrey D., *The End of Poverty*, New York, Penguin Books, 2005

Segre, Gino, *Faust in Copenhagen: A Struggle for the Soul of Physics*, New York, Penguin Group, 2007

Von Oech, Roger, *A Kick in the Seat of the Pants,* New York: Harper & Row 1986

Von Oech, Roger, *A Whack on the Side of the Head,* New York: US Game Systems, Inc. 1983

Zander, Rosamund Stone & Benjamin, *The Art of Possibility*, New York: Penguin Books 2002

3XN architects, *Investigate, Ask, Tell, Draw, Build,* London, Black Dog Publishing, 2007

ABOUT THE AUTHOR

James O. Jonassen's far-reaching leadership has helped shape the practice of architecture, helping ensure the viability and prominence of architects in tomorrow's practice models. He is recognized for his innovative approach to delivery methods and contracting vehicles, his enormous impact on health care design, and his business development and leadership.

Having served as a designer, partner, CEO, and managing partner of NBBJ for more than 40 years, Jonassen led the firm from a 100-person Seattle office to the 850-person international firm it is today, with offices in Seattle, Shanghai, Beijing, Los Angeles, San Francisco, New York, Columbus, London, Moscow, and Dubai.

His projects have received numerous design awards and have been widely published. He led teams as finalists on eight international invited design competitions, four of which they won.

Jonassen has served on the board of and chaired the health care think tank Health Insights Foundation. He served on the steering committee of two national committees of the American Institute of Architects and chaired one of them. He was a member of the AIA's Large Firm Roundtable for more than 20 years and on its executive committee for three years.

A guest lecturer at universities in Asia and North America, Jonassen has taught at the University of Hawaii for eight years. He has served on regional and national design award juries. He was awarded the Seattle AIA medal for lifetime achievement in 2008. He has been a prolific speaker on the future of architecture, practice development, and design performance. He has authored many articles on architecture, health care futures, and architectural technology.

Jonassen received his Bachelor of Architecture degree from the University of Washington and his Master of Science in Architecture from Columbia University.